Fund holding: a practice guide

Edited by
Antoinette Pirie and
Mercedes Kelly

RADCLIFFE MEDICAL PRESS
OXFORD

With the compliments of LEDERLE LABORATORIES the makers of TRAXAM (gel + foam.) & SUPRAX

15 Kings Meadow, Ferry Hinksey Road, Oxford OX2 0DP

British Library Cataloguing in Publication Data

A cataloguing record for this book is available from the British Library

Typeset by Acorn Bookwork, Salisbury
Printed in Great Britain by BPCC Wheatons Ltd, Exeter

Contents

The Authors

Nicola Amery
Fund-holding Development Manager, VAMP Health Ltd

David Colin-Thomé
Fund-holding General Practitioner, Runcorn, Cheshire

Lynne Hobden Clarke
Practice Manager, Chalfont St Peter and Editorial Adviser, *Practice Manager*

David J Horrell
Managing Director, Genisyst Ltd

Ian Howarth
Development Manager, Lincolnshire Family Health Services Authority

Mercedes Kelly
GP Fund-holding Manager, East Sussex Family Health Services Authority and SETRHA Regional Fund-holding Adviser

Paul W Lambden
Chief Executive, East Hertfordshire Trust. Former Fund-holding General Practitioner and co-founder of the National Association of Fund-holding Practices

Antoinette Pirie
Public Health Physician, North West Thames Region

Laurence Slavin
Partner, Ramsay Brown and Partners, Chartered Accountants

Ian Walker
Director of Planning and Development, Hertfordshire Family Health Services Authority

Tim Young
Partner, Bevan Ashford Solicitors, Bristol

1 Introduction

Antoinette Pirie

In January 1989 the Government published a White Paper on the future of the National Health Service (NHS), *Working for Patients*. The proposals set out represented some of the most radical changes to the NHS since its creation over 40 years ago.

A central element of the change programme is the general practice fund-holding initiative. The White Paper recognized that general practitioners (GPs) were uniquely placed to improve patients' choice of good quality services because of their relationships with patients and hospitals. The principal aim of the GP fund-holding scheme is to build on this unique situation so that patients can benefit further. It calls for the development of a management infrastructure which enables larger practices to take control of expenditure on certain services delivered to their patients. The legislation has now been passed as the National Health Service and Community Care Act 1990.

The stated objectives of the practice budget for general medical practitioners are:

- to improve the quality of services on offer to patients by GPs
- to help GPs develop their practices for the benefit of their patients
- to allow GPs greater control over the use of resources for their patients
- to encourage hospitals to be more responsive to the needs of GPs and their patients.

These aims complement the general thrust of *Working for Patients* which set out to:

- extend patient choice
- delegate responsibility to where services are provided
- secure the best value for money.

The overhaul mapped out for the NHS has several distinguishing attributes when compared to the financial and organizational structure of the NHS pre 1991:

- it offers an internal market where the provider and the purchaser of the care are separated
- it offers consumers a choice among several competing providers
- it is based on a fixed budget that encompasses both the primary and secondary care sectors
- the individual GP is offered financial incentives to provide and co-ordinate care with an eye towards resource management.

All four of these characteristics can be expected to improve efficiency. They will also provide certain incentives to improve the quality of care.

The initiative has called for a redefinition of roles and responsibilities by those involved in the delivery of health care and examination of the new working relationships that are required. To ensure success in a change exercise of this scale it has been important to ensure that:

- patients remain secure in the knowledge that health care will continue and improve
- the transitional period between existing and new arrangements is carefully planned
- the skills and expertise required to effect the change are identified and either developed or acquired.

The history of primary care as a fragmented service provided by independent contractors on the one hand, and salaried and accountable staff on the other, has ensured a lack of a coherent organizational and policy framework for developing a high quality, integrated service. The need to rationalize shared services and expand the contribution of the primary care sector in acute care reinforces the trend towards an expanded primary care service. All this has taken place within the context of an increased planning and management role for Family Health Services Authorities (FHSAs) and a White Paper which made it clear that the role of GPs is to be extended. The shifting boundaries created by the current changes within the NHS call for greater collaboration between the agencies involved in the delivery of primary health – namely FHSAs, District Health Authorities (DHAs) and independent contractors.

Realigning the boundaries between acute care and primary care is on the agenda for a number of reasons. The acute sector is increasingly concerned with maximizing throughput, reducing costs and promoting efficiency in the use of resources. In parallel with this many GPs have been keen to enhance links with the acute sector. Users of the service think that care should be provided, as far as possible, in a community setting, this is also in line with the philosophy of the World Health Organization. In practical terms this has been translated into:

- increasing the range of community-based staff to whom GPs can directly refer and work with as part of the primary care team
- increasing GP access to hospital diagnostic and therapeutic services
- increasing management of chronic disease by GPs, eg diabetes and asthma
- providing an increasing number of specialist services in a community setting.

The White Paper recognized that GPs were uniquely placed to improve patients' choice of good quality services because of their relationships with patients and hospitals. The principal aim of the GP fund-holding scheme is to build on this situation so that patients can benefit further.

Fund holding focuses on restructuring aspects of primary care and can be viewed as a lever for improving care in the hospital sector – using a bottom-up approach to effect changes throughout the entire health care system. Fund-holding practices will be making a major contribution to the overall aim of generating increased efficiency in the hospital system in the interests of patients.

Managing resources more efficiently with the goal of providing the most effective care possible within the available budget is as vital to both the patient's and society's well-being as any task now facing GPs. Who else is better able to decide whether a particular patient group is best served by more preventive, primary, secondary or long-term care? None of these are easy decisions, but with appropriate consumer input and with their knowledge of both the practice population and individual patients, GPs are in a unique position to play this role. General practice funds are a practical acknowledgement that GPs are the gatekeepers of the NHS.

2 The General Practice Fund-holding Initiative

Antoinette Pirie

The general practice fund-holding initiative is a key component of the recent changes in the NHS and in this chapter some of the main elements of the initiative are addressed. Whilst appreciating the political and philosophical arguments that surround the concept, it is not the intention to enter into that debate here, but rather to present the terms and scope of the scheme.

Which practices are eligible to become fund-holders?

Initially only those practices with at least 11,000 patients were to be considered but this has now been relaxed to 9,000. Smaller practices have been allowed to group together in order to opt for GP practice budgets.

Six pilot projects are currently underway looking at the feasibility of extending the scheme to smaller practices with list sizes of between 4,500 and 7,000 patients. It is anticipated that the limit will be relaxed in the third wave to include practices with 7,000 patients.

Practices have to demonstrate the ability to manage a budget. They need to have adequate administrative support and computer and information systems in place.

FHSAs will be responsible for the fund-holding GPs' contracts and monitor expenditure against the budget. The practices within the scheme however, will receive their budgets directly from the relevant Regional Health Authority (RHA). The Government expects close co-operation between FHSAs and RHAs in agreeing budgets with the participating practices.

Initially practice funds will be determind on a case-by-case basis taking into account the different expenditure components contributing to the total budget. In the longer term however, a universal weighted capitation formula, which reflects the actual need of a given population of patients will be used.

What is the scope of the budget?

Out of a determined annual budget the following expenditures must be covered:

- all practice team staff costs and practice accommodation costs which are at present directly reimbursed under the standard GP contract
- all expenses incurred during management of the fund and other costs associated with participation in the fund-holding initiative itself
- all drugs prescribed and dispensed
- any diagnostic investigation of patients or specimens ordered or performed by the GP (or hospital consultant, if in context)
- initial and continuing out-patient services delivered by hospital-based staff
- costs relating to a defined group of surgical in-patient and day-case treatment – the list covers most elective procedures (*see* Appendix). Emergency admissions and medical admissions are excluded
- costs relating to direct access services – at present these are limited to physiotherapy, speech therapy and occupational therapy.

It is anticipated that by 1993 the scheme will be expanded to include:

- dietetics
- chiropody
- health visiting and community nursing.

This will increase the range of services under the control of fund-holders.

A key element of fund holding is that hospitals will provide services to participating practices on a selectively contracted basis. Each fund-holding practice will negotiate its own contracts for specific services with directly managed units (DMUs), self-governing trust hospitals and/or private hospitals. There are considered to be three main types of possible contractual arrangement:

1. **Block contracts** will cover the provision of a defined block of services in return for an annual fee
2. **Cost and volume contracts** – providers will receive a defined sum for the provision of a baseline level of activity. Beyond that level, payment will be on a cost per case basis
3. **Cost per case contracts** will be payments on the basis of a sum for each case treated.

It will be necessary for practices participating in the scheme to have contractual arrangements in place prior to becoming fund-holders to ensure continuity of care.

Before the level of the budget can be agreed both the practice and the RHA will need information on current referral rates and use of hospital facilities ie laboratory and X-ray requests, attendance at out-patient departments, and surgical in-patient treatment rates. Similar information will be required during the year to monitor expenditure against the budget.

Hospitals have developed profiles of patient costs to be able to attach costs to individual treatments and procedures. They are in a position to price their services and the information will be used to permit contract funding of services.

What services are not covered in the budget?

A series of services are excluded from the budget and will be borne by the relevant DHA. These include:

- accident and emergency services
- hospital and consultant costs associated with medical cases and non-elective surgery
- maternity services
- certain preventive and screening tests
- Community Health Services.

There will be a limit to the practice's financial responsibility of £5,000 of hospital treatment per person per year. The RHA will also rescue a practice that overspends its budget by up to 5%. Expenditures in excess of this level would, however, lead to a thorough audit and the possibility of having the fund withdrawn.

3 The Decision

Paul W Lambden

Publication of *Working for Patients* fired the enthusiasm of many GPs – this was the opportunity for which many of us had been waiting. Frustration had abounded for many doctors who were unable to influence the course of their patients' care/treatment in the way that they felt was most appropriate. Patient management was governed by a range of factors over which the GP had little or no control:

- services which could easily be provided within the surgery were not provided because there was no satisfactory way of funding the costs
- services provided by DHAs were available in a blanket form when dramatic variations could be identified even within a small practice area
- care offered to patients in hospital was frequently inadequate with the views of the GP often ignored.

The GP, providing more than 90% of his patients' care, was unable to improve and expand the service across a wide range of areas, because of lack of control and inadequate resourcing.

With the reforms came the ability to influence the provision of services by making GPs the 'gatekeepers' of funding for a wide range of services. We would hold the funds for prescribing, tests and investigations, for out-patient referrals and for virtually all non-emergency surgery. Not only would this lead to increased opportunity to offer opinions but it would ensure clinical freedom to obtain the best services possible and, because funds could be vired between the various heads of expenditure, would enable GPs to prioritize their activity. This would permit, for example, a saving in the prescribing budget funding to be used in the provision of extra psychiatric counselling.

Innovation rapidly became a watchword amongst the prospective fund-holders as doctors began to examine services provided by the practice in an attempt to establish which ones could be provided more quickly, more efficiently, more cheaply and to a higher standard. As a result of this entrepreneurialism the whole character of service provision in the leading edge practices has changed; not only can patients now obtain simple services like phlebotomy, physiotherapy, counselling, ECGs and various appliances directly from the surgery, but a whole range of extended services are gradually becoming available. Increasing numbers of specialist out-patient clinics, more minor and intermediate surgical procedures and an increasing number of pathology investigations are now available at practices. The opportunities exist to expand these facilities still further and there is no reason why, in the near future, practices should not be the point of delivery for endoscopy, colposcopy, day-case local and general anaesthetic surgery, X-rays, investigations, ultrasound and a wide range of other services currently available only in a hospital setting.

Very few practices are large enough to offer all these services and it may be necessary for groups of practices to form consortia, each using available space within the practice to offer some of the services, to develop expertise and to acquire the necessary equipment for their own areas of interest. One of the greatest difficulties will revolve around the rather osteo-arthritic relationship which exists between GPs at present. Communication is poor and closer working may have been set back by the changes in the 1990 GP contract which placed increased emphasis on capitation fees thereby promoting competition.

Prescribing

The incorporation of prescribing costs in the fund has added a new dimension to the service provided by GPs. The debate over the cost of drugs has been rumbling on for several years and the advent of

PACT (Prescribing Analysis and Cost) data and, more recently, the Independent Medical Adviser, armed with an indicative prescribing budget, have been attempts to try to encourage GPs to consider more carefully the types of medication they prescribe and the costs they incur.

Nothing concentrates the mind about drug expenditure as much as being placed in charge of the money to buy those drugs and, given the extra incentive that any savings can be used to purchase care in other areas. Suddenly fund-holding practices are bristling with formularies and generic substitution has assumed a much greater importance. This can only be for the good. For too long practitioners have been using drugs for a variety of reasons, some of which do not stand up to close scrutiny. In the new order the use of a particular drug will be based on its pharmacological composition, its indications, its efficacy, its lack of side effects and its costs, and less on its advertising profile and the relationship between the doctor and the pharmaceutical company representative. In time formularies will become standard throughout general practice and the pharmaceutical company will have to market its products, either by demonstrating that they fulfil the functions of an existing formulary drug at less cost, that the side-effects of the drug are less than one which is currently used, or that the drug, although more expensive, fulfils additional functions not previously available. This will not stifle development; on the contrary it will encourage doctors to become more knowledgeable about the medication which they prescribe, encourage better communication between doctors and representatives and, at a time of increasing patient awareness and also of litigation, ensure that there is better understanding about adverse effects.

Financial benefits

The financial benefits of fund holding to GPs revolve around their ability to obtain the most effective, high quality care for the most reasonable price. There is no possibility of the GP increasing his own income under the scheme, a principle which is inviolable, and rightly so. The scheme could be open to abuse if there was any possibility of profiteering within it. It may be that a practice is able to make savings from its fund by careful husbandry of resources but, in the event of this occurring, any savings can only be spent on the purchase of additional patient care or on the acquisition of additional equipment or building for the surgery in order to expand the range of services available. Purchases of the latter type can be made only after the saving has been achieved, not prospectively in anticipation of reduced service provision costs. Savings can be accumulated for a period of up to four years before being reclaimed by the RHA. From my own knowledge of first-wave and prospective fund-holding GPs it is quite clear that their motives for wishing to be involved with the administration of their own funds is to improve services and to control more efficiently their medical activity. There is absolutely no wish to make a 'fast buck' and, combined with the safeguards, no risk that it could happen.

Control and monitoring

How is control to be maintained over GPs involved in the scheme? Here again it is important not to forget the integrity of the GPs who want to make the fund-holding initiative successful.

Computers

It is the universally held view that good quality, clear records must be kept and the lynch-pin is the fund-holder software which is now producing a standard of data unparalleled in any clinical area within the NHS. There is no doubt that the quality of the fund-holder software is such that practices are at least two years ahead of provider units, a fact which became increasingly obvious during the initial months of the scheme as hospitals struggled to generate meaningful waiting list data and information on completed in-patient and out-patient activity.

The FHSA

The information generated by the software goes to the FHSA which has been charged with the day-to-day monitoring of the scheme. It is the FHSA's function to provide an interface between the practice and the Region, collecting the necessary information, dealing with queries and difficulties, meeting the management expenses through payment of the management allowance, acting as a local inspectorate of the scheme and also promoting the fund-holding initiative to uncommitted practices within the area. Most GPs feel comfortable working with the FHSA which they have known for many years and with which they still feel able to communicate.

The Regional Health Authority

The highest level of control is mediated through the RHA whose responsibility it is to oversee all fund-holding activity within the Region. In some areas the negotiation will be via the FHSA whilst in others it will occur directly with practices. Traditionally GPs have had almost no contact with their RHA and, particularly in the early stages of fund holding, felt very suspicious about the input and requests being made. Many Regions have recognized the expediency of delegating responsibility and directing their requests through the FHSA now that mutual anxiety has been largely eliminated. This level of monitoring is essential to guarantee the integrity of the scheme and to ensure that there is no abuse, however unlikely.

1. Sensitivity to patient needs. The nature of the patient population in any practice is very variable and, even within a mile or two, there may be patient cohorts requiring completely different services. For example, in my own practice area, there is one population of largely elderly, dependent patients with no transport, who suffer from the cardiovascular and rheumatic diseases prevalent in that age group, whereas, less than a mile away, there is a separate population of affluent middle-aged patients who have private insurance, plentiful motor transport and who would have virtually no use for the services needed by the elderly group. A fund-holding GP can be sensitive to these variations in need which may be dramatic even within a small catchment area. The DHA provides its services for populations of 150,000 and above in a much more general way without sensitivity, flexibility and discrete local knowledge. It is of considerable advantage for the fund-holder to be able to deliver services with access to detailed, local population data.

Additionally the fund-holder will have negotiated his own provider unit contracts and will be aware of the agreements in terms of waiting times for out-patient consultations and in-patient episodes and for the first time will be in a position to advise the patient of anticipated delays.

2. Freedom of referral. All fund-holding GPs are entitled to refer patients to whichever hospital they choose, nationally or internationally, in their quest to obtain the most advantageous treatment. Clearly they must be able to justify the reasons for sending patients long distances or spending large sums of money on treatments but it is not unreasonable that any doctor, allocated public money, should be accountable for his actions. Recently a fund-holding GP in East Hertfordshire sent a patient to a surgeon in Cleveland for a pilonidal sinus operation. Local surgeons were perfectly competent but, in this case, the patient's family lived in Cleveland and were happy to provide post-operative care and convalescence facilities. Had the patient, who lived alone, had his operation locally, he would have required a large amount of postoperative nursing support which would have resulted in a more expensive and less efficient level of care.

3. Service provision within the surgery. The benefits of obtaining additional treatment in the surgery are self-evident. It is much more convenient for the patient, there are fewer problems with transport because ambulances are not required, the patient's medical record is available if required, the GP looking after the patient is accessible and, of course, the provision of services in the surgery is much cheaper than in a capital-charged hospital.

4. Hospital spare capacity. Many provider units have beds which are closed and theatres which are not fully utilized. Fund-holders now have the opportunity to purchase that capacity to enable their patients to obtain rapid, high-quality services without disadvantaging any patients on District waiting lists. Indeed patients of non-fund-holding practices will also benefit because the patients of fund-holders, who follow a separate track, will be removed from District waiting lists which will subsequently become shorter.

5. Use of the private sector. There are circumstances in which the best treatment for a patient could be in the private sector. This is particularly true for those procedures given a low priority by NHS hospitals, for example, female sterilization procedures, but it may also be useful if the local unit is under pressure. Furthermore there may be very reasonable financial arrangements to be made if patients are prepared to accept their operation during holiday periods when the private hospital might otherwise be under-utilized. Certainly private sector hospitals are showing increasing interest in providing services at competitive, fixed-cost prices.

6. Use of complementary medicine. There are no restrictions on fund-holders using complementary therapies for their patients and these can include acupuncture, osteopathy and homoeopathy. I recently arranged for a rheumatoid arthritic patient to obtain a course of homoeopathic injections following the failure of a comprehensive range of conventional therapies administered by several skilled rheumatologists. I am pleased to say that, for the first time in several years, he is riding his bicycle again and so, for whatever reason, the treatment has been successful and a justification of the use of public money to finance complementary medicine.

There can be little doubt that as the fund holding scheme develops and expands, the advantages to patients are becoming more apparent and fund-holding GPs are exploring more ways in which to deliver care effectively and efficiently.

Benefits for provider units

From the point of view of the critic of the reforms there are no benefits for provider units; the fund-holding arrangements do little more than add to the workload of the provider unit administration, add complications in the form of multiple contracts with purchasers (often for only small amounts of money), and introduce the concept of multiple waiting lists which are difficult to manage. Some unit managers would even say that fund-holders, by controlling the last 5–10% of a hospital's budget, actually hold the hospital to ransom, forcing it to provide treatment of an agreed standard to fund-holders that it cannot provide to other purchasers, although those purchasers may have contracts which, in cash terms, are worth much more than the fund-holding ones.

Of course, in the worst scenario, with undynamic hospital management and an uninterested consultant body, there is probably an element of truth in these suggestions. However, it is a misrepresentation of the truth in the vast majority of cases. The old system of funding hospitals on the basis of a notional catchment area was inappropriate. It provided no incentive to improve services and fostered and nurtured the 'if you don't like it, go somewhere else' attitude. Most hospitals are efficient but some are not; most consultants work very hard but some do not. The lazy doctor and the poor manager lost nothing as a result of their disinterest or lack of skill. Fund holding is the first stage in the replacement of notional funding with the concept of money moving with the patient. The more work the hospital actually does, then the more money it will receive. The better the quality of care, the more work it will attract and the more money it will receive.

Fund-holding practices examine the quality of care their local hospital is offering. Although it may strain friendships and cause distress, the fund-holder is responsible for his patients and if that means moving the work to another hospital to get better care, then that is what he must do. Hospitals that are crying foul because fund-holders have moved work away should enquire why this has happened. It is unlikely to be vindictive and much more likely to be the result of better quality being available elsewhere. Perhaps such a hospital should then examine its own service provision and put in place the improvements which will attract the work back.

Multiple contracts do not only have a nuisance value. They are valuable markers of quality, designed initially in the fund-holding round to measure basic standards of delivery of care. This is the first time that such information has been documented and it is proving innovative in giving doctors some measure of the performance that they can expect from the hospital. The sort of quality criteria which GPs have incorporated into their contracts include:

- delay between GP consultation and receipt of hospital appointment
- length of wait from referral to out-patient consultation
- length of wait from diagnosis to admission for surgery
- number of days drugs issued to patient at discharge from hospital
- basic criteria associated with discharge letter.

None of these criteria should be onerous and all should be negotiable. There is no merit in a hospital agreeing to quality standards that it cannot possibly meet – its deficiencies will be clearly shown if the contract is not met. The result will be disappointment and failure to attract work in the future. The successful hospital will meet quality specifications detailed in the contract and they will be used as a basis for negotiating for improved standards during the subsequent contract period and for continued support from the purchaser.

As new contracts are formulated, enterprising practitioners will be looking to extend the range of criteria by which the quality of care delivered by the hospital is measured. There are any number of possible indicators on which a hospital can be assessed; ranging from, for example, post-operative infection rates to whether there are flowers on the ward. Crucial although the former might be, and minor although the latter might appear, it may well be the flowers which the patient will judge as the important factor in deciding whether his stay was acceptable. This sort of assessment will open up a new area of difficulty, notably deciding on whether quality specifications should be confined to medical factors such as delays, death rates, wound infection rates, complications etc, or whether 'social' factors such as quality of food, availability of single rooms, standard of cleaning should merit equal consideration. It is the medical factors which will concern the person as a patient but the latter factors which will concern the person as a consumer.

Type of contract

In the first year of fund holding most contracts negotiated by GPs have been cost and volume contracts, with a smaller number of block contracts and cost per case contracts. Provider units will be experiencing most difficulty with the cost per case contracts because of the amount of work involved for a relatively small financial consideration. In the next few years it is likely that more cost per case contracts will be negotiated as there is increasing clarification about the exact nature of the contracts and the data associated with each patient episode becomes more accurate. For example, in the first year some hospitals have negotiated an average cost per in-patient episode operating on an average case-mix basis and, because of lack of information, new and chronic attenders have been grouped together and a price per new out-patient referral inclusive of all re-attendances and chronic attendances has been agreed. This will not continue and charges per consultation will become the normal arrangement as costing and attendance information becomes more accurate. In the near future there will be much clearer ideas about patient flows and patterns of care, and patient movements will hopefully be more streamlined as a result.

Contracts improve quality, particularly where they are negotiated with multiple providers. They introduce incentives into the provision of care, encouraging the provider unit staff to try a little harder to provide a little more in order to secure the contracts which will ensure the financial viability and the clinical activity of the unit.

Future developments

Fund-holding is the 'jewel in the crown' of the NHS reforms, the area in which most developments will occur – driven by the initiative and enthusiasm of GPs who had formerly been so frustrated at their inability to provide appropriate services for their patient populations.

One of the most crucial areas for change will be the redevelopment of the practice as health maintenance units delivering a comprehensive range of services, many of which can, at the present time, only be obtained in the hospital. The benefits are enormous. Convenience, control of provision and huge financial savings are the key factors, with the hospitals retreating in their service provision into those areas where only they can provide the services, notably for investigations requiring equipment too large or technical expertise too specialized for a practice, for operations requiring overnight stays and degrees of medical competence or monitoring beyond the scope of the practice. Attitudes of GPs to one another will have to change because it will be crucial to share services to ensure local viability. The old cottage hospital type of establishment will cease to exist, unless owned by consortia of GPs and centres of expertise in medicine or surgery in the community will form under the auspices of GPs with consultant input.

In the hospital the types and range of contracts for the provision of services will expand and increase. Quality standards will increase and pressure from GP fund-holders will ensure that progress continues. Those hospitals which can offer the types and quality of procedures which are required by GPs will develop, expanding their staff and capacities to meet the challenges presented to them. There will, of course, be casualties. Some hospitals will not be able to meet the new requirements and, as patients are diverted elsewhere, there will be a spiralling downwards with ultimate closure unless they are able to make the necessary improvements. This should be firmly regarded as a merit of the system, reductions and closures occurring because the demand is not there rather than because of some inequity in the distribution of funding from the centre. There is already some evidence to suggest that, far from destroying or emasculating the hospital service, fund holding and money moving with the patient may be the central factors in the development of a breed of high quality, high performance hospitals which will be a credit to the NHS.

4 The Preparatory Year

Mercedes Kelly

The introduction of fund holding gives GPs the opportunity to exercise direct control over NHS resources for the benefit of their patients. It is essential that the preparatory year is planned in advance to prepare for the opportunities that holding a fund gives a practice. The timetable shown below will be subject to regional variation and the responsible officers at the FHSA will advise of the local schedule.

April

As soon as the practice has received official recognition it is strongly advised that a lead GP, deputy lead GP and a fund manager form a project team. This should be the core working group who will 'cascade' information to other partners and staff as the preparatory year develops. Collection of practice activity data should begin at this stage. The analysis of this will form the basis of the Region's assessment for the practice fund. As the methodology for data collection varies in every region the responsible FHSA officer will give advice covering what data needs to be collected and how to do this, but a general rule of thumb is to capture information on everything that is referred out of the practice to provider units. There are now many computerized systems which will help with the data collection exercise. Investigate this with your local computer supplier.

May

The practice expenditure programme for the preparatory year will need to be started now as most FHSAs expect to receive it by the end of June. The earlier it is received at the FHSA the faster the practice has access to the years management allowance. So begin to plan this now. Again there are regional variations, but the majority of information required is within easy reach in your annual report. The work programme should consist of a maximum of six pages with headings and an outline expenditure of the management allowance. The FHSA will approve expenditure as soon as the programme has been received and assessed.

Guidance to work expenditure programme

Part 1: the practice population

Detail the catchment area with a brief summary of the population – demography, morbidity and special factors such as ethnicity or deprivation. At this point list any objectives that the practice may wish to achieve within the practice population. Also any tasks and actions required to achieve them, with the likely costs.

Services provided to patients

For this part of the work programme you should find the information readily available in your annual plan. Describe the services offered now, and include any clinics and activities provided. If you have plans to improve or add services which will be related to fund holding include the details here supported by action plans, costs and possible completion dates.

Part 2: the practice staff team

Much of this will be available from the practice report but you will need to expand on any additional staff required to manage the preparatory year, any special skills required and intended salaries. The costs should be included here.

Part 3: the practice premises

This information will be included in your annual report, so a brief description will suffice. If the practice intends to make any improvements, cost and plans should be included.

Part 4: data collection and information systems

This will be unique to the RHA that your practice is situated in and the local FHSA will advise you on how the data should be collected.

Part 5: medical audit activities

Describe any medical audit activities undertaken within the practice and outline your action programme for setting up systems for this and its associated costs.

Part 6: management of the fund

This section should outline the practice's major strengths and the features which will enable it to manage a fund. It should detail those who will have the authority to commission, purchase, approve and negotiate services.

Describe the systems you intend to set up to manage the fund and the associated costs.

Part 7: summary of estimated costs for preparatory work programme

Insert the total costs from each part of your work programme

Part 1	£
Part 2	£
Part 3	£
Part 4	£
Part 5	£
Part 6	£
Part 7 Estimated costs total	£

June

Following approval of the management allowance the practice can appoint a fund manager either from within the practice or outside it. Regional and/or FHSA training for GPs and senior staff begins at this time. Again the responsible FHSA officer will advise on what is available. These courses are usually accredited for the Postgraduate Education Allowance. The following are examples of what is generally available: an introduction to fund holding; modules on finance and business planning; contracting simulations, such as 'Numberside'; negotiating a health service. The practice should begin to look at starting its business plan and decide who will take responsibility for producing it. The training events will be geared to help you understand the process and help you complete the plan on schedule.

July/August

During these months the practice should be monitoring data collection, attending relevant training events and obtaining anticipated practice staffing and prescribing costs from the FHSA for use in the business plan.

September

Submission to the RHA of the business plan. Discussions between practices, DHAs and provider units commence. Around this time the providers should begin to make contact with you in anticipation of 'doing business' with your practice. The senior staff member and project group will need to set aside time for these discussions. The local provider units should be able to give you a directory with their prices and a list of contacts. Seminars for fund-holding practices continue.

October/November

The first round of visits by the RHA team begins. This will be the start of your negotiation with the Region over the fund for the practice. The practice will reap the rewards of comprehensive data collection on practice activity at this time. Good data collection will enable you to substantiate figures and aggregated numbers of patients that your Region may have. Remember that this is only the first offer and you will have time to check the figures given and cross-check with those which the practice has kept. The practice should also determine the number of patients on their main provider's waiting lists.

December/January/February

Throughout these months the choice of computer software and hardware should be made. The negotiation of the practice fund will continue during this time. The frenetic pace of the summer will have begun to slow down during these months. The lead GP and fund-holding manager will be preparing to set up contracts and negotiating for services with the main providers. The ancillary staff and prescribing costs will be firmed up with the FHSA at this point.

February

Agreement of the proposed fund and confirmation that the practice wishes to proceed to hold a fund from April.

March

The final round of negotiation with main providers and contracts signed.

1 April

Fund holding begins.

Remember that timetables for the preparatory year will vary from Region to Region. Presently, devolvement of responsibility for fund holding to FHSAs is at the top of Regional agendas, and as the FHSAs gear themselves up with resources for fund-holders, timetables will become more evident and the GP fund-holding process will begin to slot into Regional and District planning cycles.

A sample timetable for preparatory year

April/May	June	July	August	September	October	November	December	January	February	March	April
Training event - Induction Programme for Preparatory Year	**Training event -** module 2 Principle's of Financial Management-Marketing for Fundholders	**Training event -** module 3 Business Guidance Planning		**Training event -** module 4 Negotiating Skills	**Training event -** module 5 Indicative Prescribing seminar	**Training event -** module 6 Skills of contracting with Providers	**Training event -** module 7 Media Training	**Final calculation** of practice funds. Practice confirms wish to proceed with fund holding	**Final negotiation** of service agreements	**Service agreements signed**	**Fund-holding practice goes 'live'**
Module 1 Purchasing Health Care					**Meeting** with FHSA medical adviser for indicative prescribsing budgets	In house advertising for those patients who are chronic hospital attenders	**Contract discussions** with provider units	**Installation** of software system and training in its use			
Data collection begins in format requested by individual Regions with guidelines issued for collection	**Data collection** continues	**Data collection** continues	**Data collection** continues	**Data collection** continues			**Setting up service agreement**				
	Work programme devised and agreed with FHSA		**Anticipated practice staffing and prescribing costs** to be obtained from FHSA for use in business plan.	**Business plan** for submission to Region and FHSA	**Contact provider units** for practice waiting lists	**Discussions** begin with provider units.		**Negotiation** continues			
					Fundholding software and computer selection	**Initial visits** from Regions and FHSA to discuss fund allocation					

5 The Role of the FHSA

Ian Howarth

The infrastructure of the NHS is continuing to change with these changes being process driven by purchasing consortia/authorities. This may or may not affect accountability. For this chapter I am going to assume that the status quo is to be maintained with FHSAs and DHAs purchasing separately under a joint strategy but retaining a degree of competition from which service improvements and raised standards will ensue.

In order to consider how the role of the FHSA will develop in the management and operation of the general practice funding scheme, it is necessary to outline what their role was in the first wave of 1991/92.

Whilst overall responsibility for implementation of the scheme lay with the RHAs it was decided in some Regions to devolve responsibility wherever possible to the FHSAs. This was the approach adopted in Trent Region of which Lincolnshire is part, and it is from this perspective that I discuss the future of FHSAs in the management of the fund-holding scheme.

During the preparatory year the FHSA had to operate against a background of absent regulations, vague and ambiguous guidelines and time constraints. Pressure of time, however was a great propellant and acted as a positive force. It also became clear that local discretion in the absence of regulations and guidelines was required to sustain the momentum of the preparatory activity and to keep the practices 'on the boil'.

In order to maintain consistency within the Region, project managers with joint FHSA/RHA appointments were introduced and made accountable to the FHSA general manager. Meeting on a monthly basis to discuss scheme operation, and offer mutual support they acted as a conduit between the practices and the FHSA. Adopting this approach provided an ideal arrangement which meant that the RHA remained up to date with implementation progress, the FHSA had maximum involvement, gained valuable early experience and the practices enjoyed contact with a local 'friendly' face.

Initial contact

An initial assessment of the practices was conducted to ensure that they were able to satisfy the basic entry criteria and that the practices were adopting an appropriate attitude to the scheme. The Lincolnshire view was that it was better to cultivate future successful practices than maximize the number of scheme entrants. Therefore practices had to be eligible and willing to join without an FHSA 'sales drive' and be able to demonstrate good performance in terms of health targets and GP contract compliance.

It is with a certain degree of ambivalence that Lincolnshire FHSA approaches year two and beyond. Practices have to be monitored in terms of service and financial performance on the one hand and encouraged to develop initiatives and extend services on the other. These two apparently conflicting roles of the FHSA are discussed below, taking the preparation of second wave practices together with the development of first wave practices and then identifying the control and monitoring mechanisms.

Practice management

Any potential fund-holder needs to establish sound business management and a robust organizational structure. There are some very good practice managers already in post and in some cases it is possible to appoint these people to new management positions. However, a new appointment often needs to made to ensure that the right calibre of manager is in place. The FHSA should play a major role in helping to make this appointment. We have been involved in producing job descriptions, placing adverts and attending selection interviews for fund-holding managers. It is to the practices' credit that they welcome this arrangement and recognize that they are largely inexperienced in some areas at this level. New appointees should be on rolling, short-term contracts and performance-related pay should be a feature of their terms of service. Establishing this arrangement paves the way for practice management to be brought into the mainstream NHS management structure – which is an eventuality rather than a possibility.

Some practices have attempted to 'manage' by utilizing some input from an interested partner. Ultimately this is unlikely to work. The relatively steady state of year one did not test the manager-partner as they will be in the future when activity becomes more intense.

The FHSA needs to ensure that all practices preparing for scheme entry have good internal organization and at least comparative equity of funding with other similarly situated practices. The FHSA resource allocation methodologies will vary in their intricacy. It is vital that this resource allocation is completed early to identify what the effect on the general medical services (GMS) allocation to the practice is before the level of drawings on set-up fees and subsequently management fees can be established. Increases in the GMS allocation are not necessarily for management staff and could include other support staff.

Operationally, the FHSA and practice management structure can work together to institute practice policies, procedures and protocols to provide a firm operational base for the future.

Information technology

FHSAs increasingly have in-house staff to advise practices on systems suppliers, specifications and operations. Using this expertise FHSAs will be guiding practices looking to buy a fund-holder system. Each system is modelled on the Department of Health specification with the differences between models being mainly due to user demand for amendments. Practices ought to remember that in buying a system they are buying a companys' service too. Therefore it is very important to examine 'helpline' response rates and other after-sales service quality.

In the longer term, FHSAs will be looking towards electronic links with practices. Some of the links currently reported are little more than electronic mailing links. At this stage links might include, monthly financial out-turns and ad-hoc enquiries by the FHSA on the fund-holder system into contracts or budget performance. FHSAs are already considering how they might reduce the paper transfer between themselves and fund-holders; fax links, floppy disks and modems are currently being investigated.

Business planning

The business plans of the first wave practices were a brave attempt but were largely introspective and philosophical. It was an unreal situation with practices guessing what the potential for savings was, the fund offers being some months away.

Using the first wave fund offers as a benchmark, future fund-holding practices will have to produce plans that are more analytical and objective. The plans need to be valid working documents which map out all future activity.

The FHSA and DHA both have to submit their own business plans to the RHA and are subject to formal review. It seems a logical progression for this arrangement to be carried down to practice level. Progress and development in the future will be driven by structural planning and review. FHSAs would have, at least at this stage, to protect relationships with practices by conducting the reviews without being intrusive.

Fund-holders may be wary of such a review process and many would consider it to be an infringement of their right to manage their own resources. However, this argument cannot be sustained because as drawers from the public purse practices are no less accountable than the public authorities for good financial management.

Contracting

The process of contracting in the first wave was hampered by uncertainty, lack of even semi-accurate costings and the tardiness that existed between units and DHAs. For the future waves, the contracting process is not initially dependent on accurate activity data. Even in the early stages practices should have identified what their expectations are of contract content in terms of treatment and patient processing.

The FHSA clearly needs to be involved in the contracting process for several reasons. Firstly, the FHSA can guide the practice on whether the conditions or terms they seek are allowable, ethical and possible. Secondly, the FHSA by being involved can facilitate negotiations to some extent and help bring the two parties closer together.

It is essential for health managers to be aware of contracting intentions so that the effects of market forces on patient care and local services can be anticipated. Local priorities and strategies have to be recognized in the contracting process. This is particularly relevant if GPs start to examine the scope for casting a wider net in search of providers.

A natural advance, is the contract which brings consultants in to the surgery and enables consultant services to be bought on a private basis. The benefits here are a local service with GP input and savings on the fund, with a more efficient service provided in terms of access time and cost. The RHA, through the FHSA, will monitor contracts where the practice has established a private company to act as broker.

Ultimately, the contracting process is based on quantified patient flows, treatment and outcomes; and practices should not underestimate the need for accurate, detailed and meaningful data. In addition, the practice should be working with the FHSA to obtain data from their DHA and providers on what is happening locally. There will be disparities and these will need to be investigated. Remember too much data can be trimmed or discarded, too little will reduce the fund offer, or at the very least leave the practice ill-prepared. In these circumstances practices' contracting confidence will be limited, pushing the fund-holder towards block contracts or cost and volume contracts with a high percentage block element.

The term contracting ought to mean that purchasers, fund-holders in this case, are adopting a truly commercial manner in securing agreements for their patients' treatments. However, apart from a few isolated instances, producing comparatively small benefits, fund-holders have behaved similarly to DHAs in that the existence of a contract was an end in itself.

FHSAs have a major role to play in the future as commissioning agents. In a small way this was their role in the first wave of contract discussions but dialogue revolved around quality issues like waiting times in out-patient clinics or whether a discharge letter could be faxed within 24 hours. Within this role there will be a need for the FHSA to monitor services in terms of providers' compliance to contracts with fund-holders and to identify areas of subsequent or even in-year improvement in performance. Building up a knowledge base will give a clear view to the FHSA of what the non-GP-fund-holder should expect to be reflected in local service agreements between the DHA and providers at the round of drafting service agreements. It is recognized that it will be the fund-holders who establish new and raised standards with each round of negotiations. FHSAs will then need to bring together the DHAs, the providers and the non-fund-holder to institute these standards generally.

Monitoring arrangements

The control mechanisms on fund-holding practices are placed early in the preparatory year and, all working procedures, protocols and computer operations have to reflect standards which will satisfy an audit exercise.

Subsequently, practices in the preparatory year will need to produce an expenditure plan for the set up/management fees and secure agreement from the FHSA to proceed. Practices should bear in mind that the set up fee/management fee is available by agreement and not an automatic entitlement. FHSAs have a responsibility to ensure that value for money is obtained whilst at the same time using local discretion and common sense in pursuit of progress.

Once the practice is operationally tied into the scheme and in addition to the planning review of the practice and personal performance review of the manager, there will be the financial controls which monitor the practice monthly out-turns. FHSAs are preparing themselves to effectively use these documents for routine monitoring and to intervene where appropriate.

Various publications and guidance letters have discussed 'mismanagement' by practices but it is clearly an FHSA's responsibility to anticipate and redress problems. There could be cases where preventive action could not have been taken and the FHSA will then have a damage limitation role. Continuance of the scheme in both cases is for the RHA to decide upon, with advice from the FHSA. The regulations are not comprehensive enough to cover all eventualities ie termination of combined fund operation by one or more practices, on partner death for example, and therefore a contingency policy document which anticipates these circumstances needs to be developed and accepted locally.

Fund holding is a journey, not a destination. FHSAs are acting with the practice as catalyst, facilitator and regulator until the practice is confident enough to make its own way. As mentioned previously the Lincolnshire perspective is to nurture success and build upon it. This can only come from the practice and the FHSA working closely together at every stage. This, above all, is the key message that I would pass on and in the first year of the scheme much of the feedback from other regions reinforces this approach.

6 The Fund-holding Manager

Lynne Hobden-Clarke

A budget is given to fund-holding practices, which they use to buy hospital services, pay practice staff and pay for the drugs they prescribe. The actual management of the fund can be quite daunting to the average practice and a new breed of manager, fund-holding managers, has emerged to take this pressure from doctors.

What skills does the new manager need?

The fund manager need not be specially recruited – they may be the existing practice manager or someone already working in the practice. The basic management skills required are those of communication, team building, organizational and training ability linked with financial awareness, computer literacy, statistics and an understanding of negotiating contracts. Some practice managers will relish the opportunity of a challenge and will be willing to attend training to enhance their financial planning and monitoring skills. Some will plead, quite rightly, that practice management is already a full time role and there is no room for another major responsibility. For these reasons many practices choose to recruit a person from the business world. There is no doubt that a business background will provide many of the additional skills required to run a fund, however, these can also be present in a well-motivated practice manager.

There is no right or wrong choice, it will depend entirely upon the views and resources of each individual practice.

The implications of using an existing manager

The whole practice staffing and reporting procedures will need to be reviewed to allow for the dual role. Routine duties will need to be delegated to a deputy to create time for managing the fund and secretarial time may also be needed to remove some of the burden of administration and deal with correspondence. A data entry clerk is essential to feed patient activity information into the fund-holding software. To pay a manager to do this would be a shameful waste of resources. Although fund holding is quite separate in administrative terms, the ability to take an overview and translate fund-holding decisions into implications for the practice is a definite advantage.

The implications of recruiting a manager

The alternative to using an existing manager is to recruit a manager for fund holding. How do you find such a person, and what constitutes 'relevant experience'? Initially, there was a lot of publicity about needing someone with an accounting background. Lately this has shifted in emphasis to 'entrepreneurial' skills. This suggests that to have held a senior post in a profit-making organization would be suitable.

The greatest dangers lie in the selection procedure. It is imperative that the partners have a clear idea of the role they expect, and to be agreed upon it. To formulate a job description crystallizes thoughts and will bring differing perceptions to light. There may be conflict in the roles of the practice manager and the fund manager, and the job descriptions of both can be dovetailed before the new person arrives. The existing practice manager must be involved in formulating the job descriptions, and be quite clear about the partners reasons for splitting the management responsibilities. The job titles should convey the function, for example 'business manager', 'fund manager' or 'operations manager'. Avoid using ambiguous terms, for example 'executive manager'.

Practice implications

Staff

The implications on the practice staff need to be evaluated, and some reassurance may be necessary. Try producing a chart showing each person's position and the reporting procedure. The staff will need to be informed about the new structure and the possibility of additional staff for fund holding. It is a good idea to invite staff to apply for the new posts, again reducing the general resistance to such a major change. *See* Figures 6.1 and 6.2.

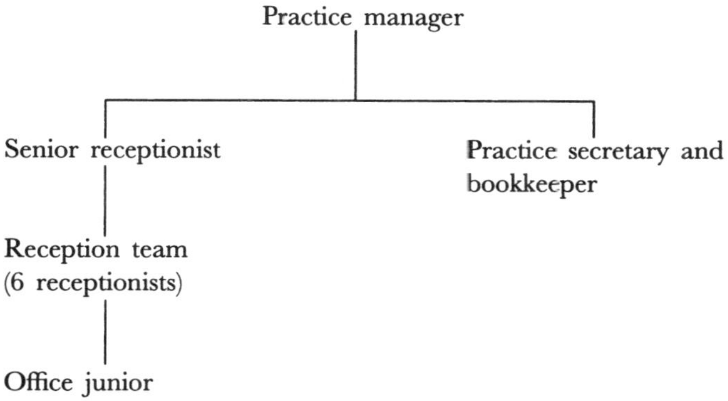

Figure 6.1: Staffing structure before fund holding.

No matter how the fund is going to be managed there is an inevitable increase in staff, either recruited specifically for fund holding or by restructuring the practice to release time for fund holding, or both. The impact on the practice expenses needs to be costed, although some of the additional staff can be paid from the management fee. This has the advantage of being a 100% reimbursed instead of the usual 70%.

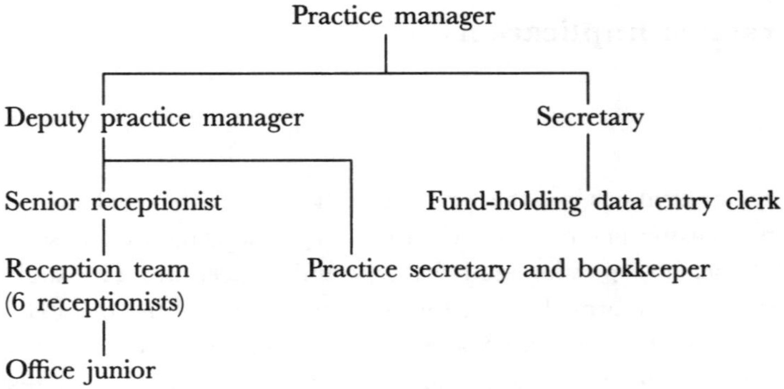

Figure 6.2a: Using the existing practice manager to manage the fund-holding practice.

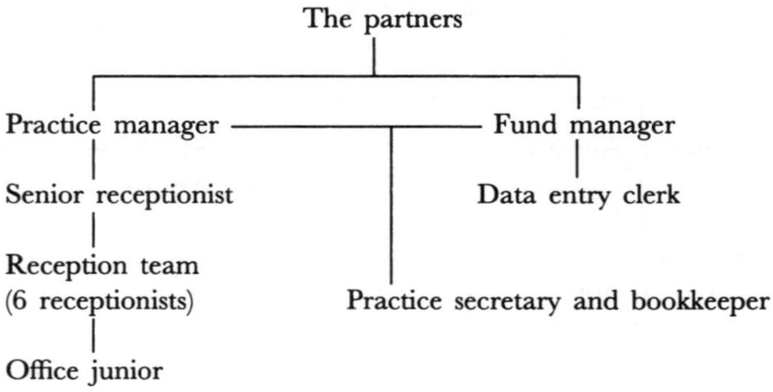

Figure 6.2b: Recruiting a fund manager.

Space

Where will all these people work, and is there enough space for the additional computers to run the software? Most premises are already in dire need of administrative space and this may precipitate some necessary extensions or alterations. Again, help may be at hand from the FHSA in the shape of an improvement grant.

Communication

Fund holding has a general impact on the overall standards of communication within the practice. The doctors must pass the details of each referral, investigation and X-ray ordered to the fund manager or data entry clerk. As time progresses and freedom to place contracts increases the partners must also have some agreement about the consultants to whom they refer, and why. In most practices referral options have been quite personal and not even discussed with colleagues. Suddenly not only the doctors' views, but those of patients, need to be included in the equation. Patient questionnaires about the service that they have received, either as an out-patient or an in-patient, are part of the evaluation process. Not only should they include questions like 'did the consultant explain clearly what was wrong?', but 'was the waiting area clean and pleasant?', and 'did you feel there were enough nurses available?'. The fund manager must collate all these comments and be able to present them to the partners when the time for placing contracts comes around.

Time must be set aside for regular partnership meetings to be devoted exclusively to managing the fund and the contracts. Also for staff training to keep them up to date with practice policies and preferences. In addition, there are many meetings with other agencies, for example the FHSA, RHA, local hospital managers and consultants, all of which will take time away from the patients. The fund manager should have the correct skills to be able to participate in all of these meetings and possibly attend them alone if a partner is unavailable.

Therefore the fund manager must be a good communicator and have the ability to facilitate these types of discussions.

Salaries

So what should this 'supermanager' be paid? The Whitley Council scale descriptions suggest Grade 8 'a practice manager with a range of complex duties requiring investigations, recommendations and actions; or Grade 9 'a practice manager with a range of complex duties and responsibility for introducing new systems and making policy input'. This places the range of salary between £20,575 and £27,077 per annum. To attract an experienced manager from the business world, or to stop your own practice manger leaving for another fund-holding practice these salaries are essential!

Conclusion

The fund manager cannot work in isolation. Many fund-holding decisions have an impact on the general running and organization of the practice, and practice policies have an impact on fund holding. It does not matter if the management is one role or subdivided into two, communication must be strong. It will help considerably if a partner takes on the executive responsibility for fund holding. Not only is some clinical input invaluable, but also for the balance and rationalization of views of partners, managers and staff.

In conclusion, the skills required of a fund-holding manager are exactly the same as a competent practice manager.

7 Business Planning in General Practice

Antoinette Pirie

There are three fundamental components of the management task which apply in any organization:

- policy decisions
- strategy decisions
- operational decisions.

Policy decisions

Addressing practice policy requires an insight into the forces that motivate practice members and the values and principles that make them want to be in the 'business' of primary health care delivery.

In general practice the policy issues tend to get built-in and are assumed to be self-evident. Taking time to turn implicit assumptions into explicit ideas can go a long way towards deriving a focus for the practice. No group can act effectively without a clear direction and it is the partner's responsibility to involve all members of the practice team at this level in the decision-making process.

Strategy decisions

Strategy is concerned with the broad brush strokes of how to put these visions into effect. Strategic considerations should address the following issues:

- The scope of a practices' activities – does (and should) the practice concentrate on one area of activity, or does it have many? Should it contemplate a wider role in the provision of health services, for example, alternative medicine? This analysis is essential as it concerns the way in which those responsible for managing the practice view its boundaries.
- Matching the activities of the practice to the environment in which it operates.
- Matching the practice activities to its resource capability – strategy is not just about countering environmental threats and taking advantage of environmental opportunities, it is also about matching organizational resources to these threats and opportunities. There would be little point in trying to take advantage of some new opportunity if the resources needed were not available, could not be made available or it if the strategy was rooted in an inadequate resource base.
- The values and expectations of those who have power in the practice. In some respects strategy can be regarded as the reflection of the attitudes and beliefs of those with the most influence in the organization.
- The direction in which the practice is moving in the long term.
- The implications for change throughout the practice.

Operational decisions

In the next phase the broad strategic plans are elaborated into specific programmes for every day operational tasks, to 'keep the show on the road'.

Business planning

The business plan can be regarded as a means of expressing the practice policy, strategy and operational decisions in a form which can be used by management. A clear and systematic approach to business planning is central to the successful running of any business.

Aims of a business plan

- To set:
  - goals
  - targets
  - milestones.
- To measure achievement against a plan.
- To structure and record the planning process
  - identification of options
  - evaluation of options.
- To demonstrate commitment and agreement.
- To provide a business management tool for:
  - control
  - feedback
  - delegation
  - accountability.

Preparing a business plan will provide an insight into the planning process. It is actually this process which is important to the long term health of any organization and not simply the plan that emerges from it. Practices are dynamic, as are the environments in which they operate. No one expects every event recorded in the plan to occur as predicted but the understanding and knowledge created by the process of business planning will prepare the practice for any changes it may face and so enable it to adjust swiftly.

A business plan should be regarded as a key management tool, it should attempt to answer these questions:

- where do you want the practice to be in five years time?
- how are you going to achieve it?
- will the proposed plan work?

There are a number of alternative approaches to business planning but most are essentially composed of the same stages:

- definition of objectives and a statement of values
- evaluation of current position and internal assessment
- review of external environment
- preparation of practice strategy
- financial forecasts
- preparation of an action plan.

Figure 7.1: The planning hierarchy.

Definition of objectives and statement of values

The practice needs a clear identity, an agreement on mission and a statement of aims. This will involve an assessment of the past and intentions for the future. It can be regarded as a reappraisal and reaffirmation of goals. What is hoped to be achieved in the short and long-term for the practice as a whole, for the individual practice members and for the patients served? *See* Figure 7.2.

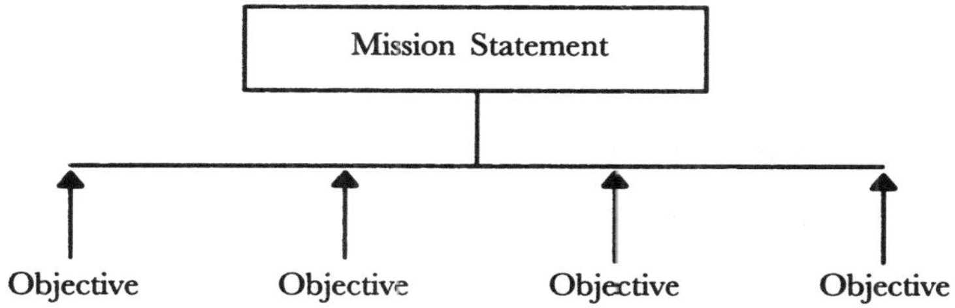

- Official goals
- Unofficial goals
- Measurable objectives

Figure 7.2: Definition of objectives.

These concepts can be encapsulated in a mission statement. The mission should be narrow enough to give direction and guidance to everyone in the practice, but wide enough to allow growth and realization of potential. Above all mission statements should be realistic, achievable and brief.

> **'A mission statement should identify what you want your practice to be doing. This may differ from what it is doing now.'** A well-defined mission statement that challenges your practice will provide the focus for the rest of the business planning process.

Evaluation of current position and internal assessment

This analysis should concentrate on strengths and weaknesses within the practice. What is done well and what is done badly? Are there any obvious reasons why?

Frankness and honesty can be difficult, as can keeping to a timetable during the whole planning process, so an outside facilitator can be invaluable at this stage. An independent assessor is also far more likely to be impartial and less prone to let personalities interfere. Some aspects of the practice that should be covered at this stage include:

- List details.
- Clinical and non-clinical services offered.
- Patients' perception of service.
- Staff profile – job descriptions
– staff skills.
- Practice management – organization structure
– lines of reporting
– management expertise
– skill deficits.
- Practice premises.
- Computer activities and support.
- Activity levels – surgery hours
– specialty clinics
– targets.
- Referral data.
- Prescribing data.
- Financial management.

Looking at these and other issues, depending on individual practices, it will be possible to derive a practice profile which highlights particular strengths and elucidates any weaknesses.

Carry out an external assessment

The overall aim in this part of the evaluation is to identify opportunities for the practice and target any potential threats. Areas that should be addressed include:

- List trends, both short and long-term.
- Local growth/contraction factors – housing developments, business relocation.
- Demographic trends in relation to the practice – location of retirement homes in the area, for example.
- A broad view of the competition – conventional and alternative. A practice does not operate in isolation and a business plan cannot be compiled without reference to other practices and agencies. Are they in competition or would collaboration be a good idea?
- The relationship with the FHSA, DHA and RHA needs to be examined and developed if necessary.

Grouped together the above analyses are often referred to as a SWOT analysis (strengths, weaknesses, opportunities, threats).

Preparation of a practice strategy

Once the practices' overall position is known it's possible to begin drawing up specific strategies to maximize progress. The aim should be to build on the strengths and eradicate the weaknesses that have been determined during the preceding analysis.

During this stage of the planning process attention should be turned to the issues that the practice has to get right to be successful and, in this new environment, to survive. These are referred to as Critical Success Factors and can range from computer capacity to links with a provider unit.

Look at where you want the practice to be in three or five years time. Objectives reflect not only what you want the practice to achieve but also what you think it can achieve. Some will fall out of the practice analysis that you have produced. For most practices, the objectives will be concerned with patient service, financial performance and with future plans for staff and premises.

Objectives must be:

- quantifiable
- within a defined time scale, and
- realistic and achievable.

If your objectives fulfil these three criteria, they will serve as useful goals and yardsticks against which to judge your performance. They will help you monitor the progress and the achievements of your practice.

Financial forecasts

Practices will need to prepare the following financial statements for two years:

- profit and loss account
- cash flow forecast
- balance sheet.

Year 1: monthly profit and loss and cash flow projections.
Year 2: quarterly profit and loss and cash flow projections.

Balance sheets should be produced at the end of each financial year.

The use of computerized spreadsheets in developing financial projections can make the whole process much simpler, particularly when performing a 'what if' analysis.

Preparation of a detailed action plan

Aims and strategies have to be turned into systems for running the practice and to ensure the improvement of health care for patients. Business plans do not implement themselves, therefore, a detailed plan of action needs to be drawn up to ensure that the planned outcome actually occurs. It will need to address:

- the tasks that need to be performed
- individual responsibilities for the tasks
- timescales involved
- quality measurements.

Many potential fund-holders will have been asked to prepare a practice business plan by the RHA as part of their application to join the fund-holding scheme. For many it will have involved a lot of extra work in an already tight schedule with little understanding of its relevance. Once drawn up, however, a business plan can be used on a working basis as a framework with which to manage all aspects of the practice. *See* Figure 7.3.

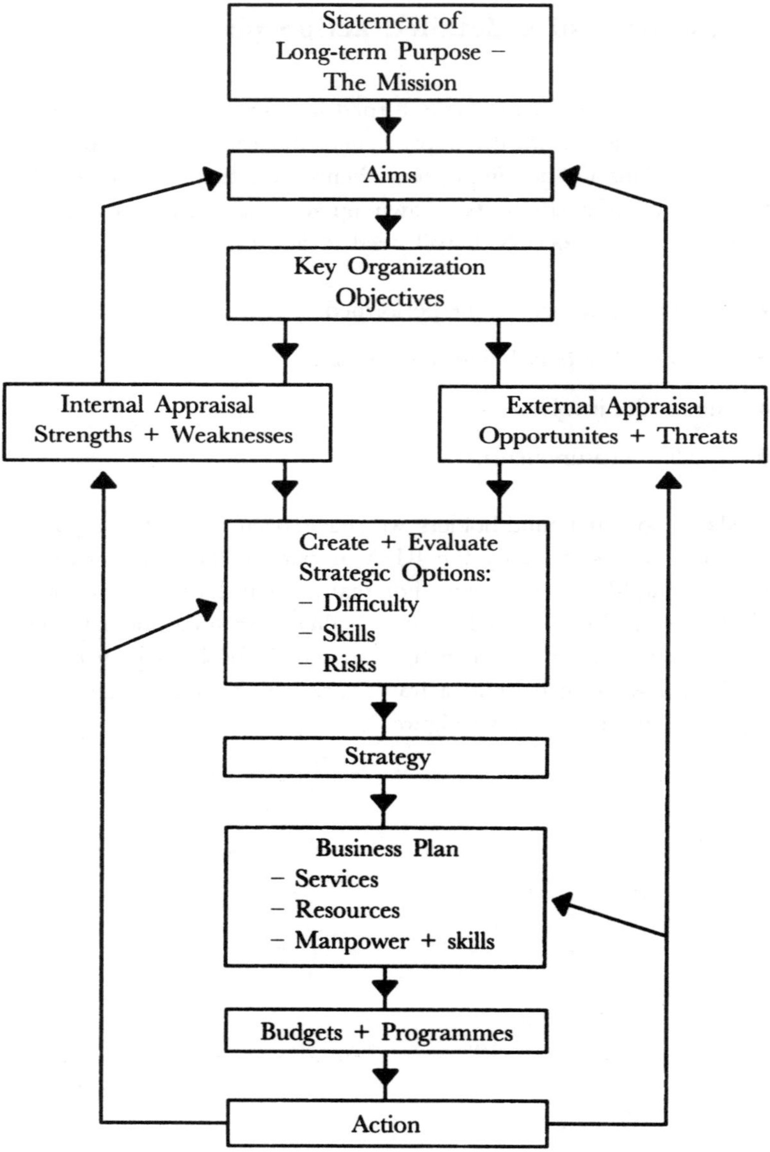

Figure 7.3: Business planning process.

8 Contracting for General Practice Fund-holders

Antoinette Pirie

NHS contracts are the means through which purchasers and providers of health care will agree on the required quality, quantity and cost of the services to be provided for their population. Using contracts as a focus for raising standards is perhaps the key objective behind their introduction.

The contracting environment

The proposals for contractual funding of hospital and community health services are designed to promote efficiency and enhance consumer choice.

- **The benefit for purchasers** (GP fund-holders and DHAs) is that they can seek to meet the health care needs of their resident populations in a way which makes the most cost-beneficial use of their resources.
- **The benefit for providers** is that services can be planned to operate at the most efficient level by attracting funding from a number of different purchasers in direct relation to the level of activity.

The purchasing role will enable DHAs and fund-holders to specify much more precisely than in the past exactly what services they aim to secure for their populations and the way those services are provided. Commissioning agencies will need to ensure that their priorities and the service agreements they enter into truly reflect the health needs of their given population. Furthermore the providers of health care will be challenged to provide services at a given level of quality and cost.

Moving to contractual funding has lead to new responsibilities and relationships for those involved. This section briefly outlines the basics of the different roles of the agencies involved.

The role of the Regional Health Authority

- To provide a strategic framework within which contracts agreed reflect the RHA's priorities in terms of overall equitable distribution of resources.
- To facilitate the contracting environment by ensuring a smooth process of reaching contracts and service agreements.
- To provide a conciliation service.
- To maintain a dialogue with purchasers, in particular GP fund-holders.
- To review/monitor plans for the use of funds in relation to overall DHA assessment of need.

The role of the District Health Authority

DHAs have moved away from planning services and managing their delivery towards identifying the service requirements of a resident population and planning and managing their purchase.

Their new tasks include:

- securing contracts which best reflect the health needs of the population for which they are responsible
- ensuring that their population has good access to a comprehensive range of high quality, value for money, hospital and community health services

- satisfying themselves that they are placing contracts in line with GP's referral preferences, and have in place arrangements to handle any extra-contractual referrals.

The main process for meeting these responsibilities is the specification of services required and negotiation of appropriate contracts.

The role of the Family Health Services Authority

- To determine priorities for meeting health care needs alongside the DHA.
- To develop a brokerage role by representing GP fund-holders and non-fund-holders in discussions about developing contracts with DHAs and provider units.
- To work with DHAs to ensure that contracting decisions satisfy GP referral patterns.
- To monitor non-fund-holding GP referrals against contracts and GP expenditure against indicative allocations.
- To determine the limitations on non-fund-holding GPs making extra-contractual referrals in consultation with DHAs and the Local Medical Committee (LMC).

The role of fund-holding GPs

Part of the DHA's responsibilities for securing services have been taken over by practices which hold practice funds.

The fund-holding practices need:

- to identify the health needs of their practice population
- to negotiate, place and monitor contracts with appropriate providers
- to maintain a dialogue with the RHA via the FHSA
- to produce annual fund-holding accounts for the FHSA.

The role of non-fund-holding GPs

- To link in with the work of the DHA on the identification of health needs.
- To identify health needs within their practice population.
- To link in with the DHA network for the agreement and monitoring of contracts.

The role of the provider unit

In the past provider units could expect an assured level of funding from one major source but had to restrict their activity level to match this. Now their level of activity is chiefly constrained by their ability to attract contract funding from purchasers. Providers will need to keep in close touch with the plans of their major purchasers and so be able to anticipate the services they will require in the future. Many will also want to widen their range of 'customers'. Provider units will wish to ensure that referring GPs are happy with the services provided, in view of the central role which GPs play in determining the pattern of referrals.

Managers of health care units will move away from delivering services within the policies and budget of a particular authority towards delivering contracted services within quantity and quality specifications to a number of clients in return for agreed levels of income. In effect their task is:

- to attract contracts from purchasers in order to ensure their viability
- to provide services at agreed levels of quality and cost.

GP fund-holders will be contracting with:

- directly managed units (DMUs)
- NHS trusts
- the private sector.

Units have drawn up descriptions of their services (a prospectus) to help ensure that potential purchasers are aware of what is on offer and can compare this with offers from other purchasers.

The contracting process

The roles and relationships outlined above enable the development of a contracting process – namely service specification, supply proposal, negotiation and review. The approach to contracts arises out of the roles and responsibilities of the purchasers and the suppliers, and concentrates on service specification and standards of service as two essential components of the contractual process.

The steps of the contracting process for GP fund-holders.

1. Identification of treatment patterns for services covered by the fund, including levels of activity and location.
2. Discussion of proposed referral patterns with the RHA/FHSA.
3. Discussions with provider units about possible terms of contracts, eg prices.
4. Discussion with the RHA about the level of funding necessary to lay contracts for hospital services.
5. Entering into provisional contracts with provider units.
6. Final commitment to contract after decision to run a fund.

Purchasers will be responsible for specifying their requirements for a given period of time. In the case of fund-holders, one year. This analysis will be based on priorities, local epidemiological forecasts and historical referral data. A practice needs assessment and anticipated changes in requirements can be regarded as the first essential step towards drawing up a service agreement. Fund-holding practices will need to set out their requirements for each of the services for which they are going to contract. The purchaser's requirement statements will be free-standing documents to be offered to suppliers for them to respond to with supply proposals. A number of Regions have helped to formalize this process by issuing guideline 'service requirements'.

GPs will need to ask themselves:

- are we happy with the current service?
- which areas need changing and which do not?
- what are our priorities for change?
- what are realistic targets to aim for (both short-term and long-term).

Choosing between suppliers

The service requirements can be offered to more than one supplier with the supply proposals being used as the basis for choice. It is, however, not suggested that anything approaching a full-blown competitive tendering exercise is entered into. There will be circumstances where there is only one possible supplier. In other cases the purchaser's knowledge of potential suppliers may mean that, subject to satisfactory supply proposals, they may be content to use their existing supplier and do not need to invite competing proposals.

Where a choice between suppliers needs to be made that judgment should not be on comparative cost alone, but rather on efficiency and quality as well.

Arriving at contracts: negotiation and agreement

Contracts will in effect, if not literally, be an amalgamation of the service requirement and the relevant supply proposal, modified as required by discussion and negotiation between the purchaser and the supplier.

Content of the contract

The contractual process should cover all aspects of the services to be provided and the expectation of both parties. A fundamental merit of contractual funding is the stimulation it gives to a much better articulation of what health service providers are expected to achieve. A service agreement or contract as a minimum should specify:

- the nature and amount of services to be provided (the approach adopted will depend to an extent on the type of contract in question)
- duration of the contract
- general or specific population characteristics (particularly relevant to block contracts)
- volumes and prices
- facilities that will be employed
- staffing requirements
- confidentiality
- the criteria for admission and discharge of in-patients and for day/out-patient referrals (a different approach needed depending on the contract type)
- the speed with which patients will get access to services and the approach to prioritization
- other quality measures to be applied
- responsibility for tertiary referrals
- subcontracting
- responsibility for clinical complications
- information the parties will make available to each other (this will include, where appropriate, nationally agreed minimum data sets)
- means of monitoring the contract, including access to premises and data
- payment schedules
- mechanics of billing, authorization and settlement.

Attached to the broad service agreements will be more detailed individual service specifications which have been agreed between the purchaser and the provider.

As expected the service agreements in the first round of contracts have largely been statements of present activity, not least because of time and data limitations. It is important however that service specifications contribute to the way in which contracts can offer a focus for raising standards and describe what, resources permitting, services should be. The way in which these can come together, and be related to what services will cost and the resources available, is an essential part of the process by which the initial service specification is translated, in negotiation with suppliers, into the actual agreement.

Choice of contract type

There are three main contract types in operation:

- block
- cost and volume
- cost per case

with possible hybrids of the three. *See* Figure 8.1.

The decision on which type to use depends on a range of factors, including:

- availability of information on which to base negotiations
- objectives and incentives inherent in different types of contract
- the volume of services to be purchased
- cost of contracting, including negotiation and monitoring costs
- the presence or lack of competition.

	Block	Cost and volume	Cost per case
Specification	Defined population	Volume level	Individual cases
Limit	Open ended	Specified volume	Provider capacity OR purchaser priorities
Effect of under-utilization	Provider surplus/ Purchaser wastage	Provider surplus/ Purchaser wastage	Purchaser could redeploy funds
Implementation	Easy to roll forward	Need to set level	Detailed costing
Monitoring information	Patient residence only	Patient residence and type of procedure	Diagnosis and/or procedure in detail
Monitoring costs	Low	Medium	High
Checks against volume	None except residence	Tally numbers against list	Tally numbers against maxima
Flexibility	Low	Medium	High
Price relative to cost	High	Medium	Low (marginal), given fixed costs covered

Figure 8.1: Choice of contract type.

Block contracts

The block contract covers access to a defined range of services at the provider unit in return for an annual fee payable in monthly instalments. The provider will need information on the approximate level of demand from the purchaser.

In using block contracts there is the risk of paying for services which prove to be unnecessary and which could lock up a significant proportion of a relatively small budget. The number of patients which individual fund-holders will be referring will be small when compared with the DHA and block contracts will not cater for the variations in need which will occur amongst a smaller pool of patients. Block contracts may, however, be suitable for practices purchasing as a consortium or where the data on treatment rates is not yet well established.

A developmental approach is essential. The contracts first let in 1991/92 have been relatively crude. That need not matter, provided those contracts can be refined at each contract review. While the direction for refinement does need to be clear, it may be of value that improvements follow from actual experience. An approach that attempted to reach an 'ideal' position at one step would be more likely to result in contracts which were either over-complicated or much too relaxed.

With experience all contracts will become more specific. Eventually block contracts may be as well defined as cost and volume and cost per case. However, the continuing distinction will be that, although they will be negotiated in the context of forecasts about the likely volume of patients to be treated, block contracts are essentially about purchasing access to facilities, rather than a defined baseline of cases or treatments. They will therefore have the advantage that they allow providers more flexibility in coping with demand, but the disadvantage that they define less precisely what is being purchased for the price. For this reason it is likely that many providers and purchasers will wish to begin with a majority of block contracts for their services and move to cost and volume agreements when and where this is possible. It is also likely that some services will always need to be provided under block contracts.

Advantages

- Closest to pre-91 practice.
- Least demanding on activity information.
- Maximum flexibility for the provider.

Disadvantages

- Getting the incentives right – providers obligations are limited – purchaser may pay for unused capacity.
- Demand may be unpredictable and therefore present difficulties for the provider.
- Difficulties in making service and quality requirements explicit.

These problems may make it necessary to develop costly monitoring mechanisms to secure quality and efficiency particularly where competition is limited. There may be a case for developing a hybrid form of block contract ie building in a workload agreement. These developments begin to relate activity to payment and incentives can be built in.

Cost and volume contracts

Cost and volume contracts specify the number of treatments or procedures to be provided for a specific price. The fixed element is also payable in monthly instalments.

Cost and volume contracts are likely to prove more useful to fund-holders. They have data collected through the practice records which will provide figures for the incidence of particular disorders and procedures and enable them to specify what they might require for a fixed fee. Cost and volume contracts can also provide the flexibility to meet variations in need for services, since they can be arranged for a set level of procedures with the possibility of exceeding that number if necessary. Cost and volume contracts have the capacity to cover a range of procedures for which an average price has been set. This type of contract could be used, for example, for the majority of surgical procedures covered by the fund.

Advantages

- Links payment with activity and maintains financial control – incentives right for the purchaser.

- Financial security for the provider but greater flexibility than with the other two types of contract.

Disadvantages

- Detailed information requirements for costing, monitoring and invoicing related to the costs of specificity.
- Purchaser wastes resources if money is committed to a fixed volume of treatments and these are not fully used.
- Costs of negotiation.

Cost per case contracts

Arranged on a price per case basis. A cost per case contract should probably be reserved for 'one-off' or small volume contracts, perhaps in circumstances where the costs of treatment warrant separate pricing. These contracts are likely to be used more by fund-holders than DHAs, because of the smaller scale of their contracting exercise.

Apart from their particular value for purchasing treatments which are less common in the smaller populations dealt with by fund-holders, they can give fund-holders the ability to purchase treatments more cheaply or more quickly using the marginal costing and capacity principles. These principles mean that fund-holders might be able to negotiate with the provider units to supply treatment for individual patients using any unanticipated spare capacity which the units might have in a year. There is a risk of the service not being available. If fund-holders are looking to 'spot buy' they need to ascertain from the provider the likely scope for in-year 'spot buying' and probably reserve it for a limited range of procedures.

Disadvantages

- High transaction costs.
- Detailed information costs.

Most suitable for:

- rare one-off cases
- part of a variable volume agreement added on to a cost and volume contract
- 'spot buys'.

Contract options

Fund-holders will have to contract for:

- certain in-patient and day-case procedures (*see* Appendix)
- all out-patient attendances except antenatal, neonatal and genitourinary clinics
- direct access for: physiotherapy, speech therapy and occupational therapy
- direct access for pathology services and X-rays
- domiciliary consultations.

The contracts fund-holders will place can relate to each area separately or various combinations.

All initial out-patient referrals are covered by the scheme and fund-holders will be able to choose whether to lay contracts for out-patient diagnosis and advice alone, or for diagnosis and appropriate treatment arising from the initial referral. To an extent the type of contract will depend on the way in which prices for out-patient referrals are quoted.

With medical conditions, where GPs are more likely to be referring for diagnosis and advice on condition management, a contract which covered all initial out-patient appointments for a particular speciality might be appropriate.

Surgical procedures, general and otherwise, on the list of in-patient treatments covered by the fund are amongst those commonly seen by larger practices. Fund-holders should be in a good position to predict the likely outcome of the out-patient referral for many of these cases. Some of the surgical procedures may lend themselves to an 'all-in' contract which specifies out-patient appointment, in-patient treatment and follow-up care.

It is recommended that contracts include procedures for informing GPs if the treatment differs from that specified in the contract although it is assumed that fund-holders will normally wish to refer patients on the basis that the provider will carry out whatever treatment is needed without further authorization from the practice.

The price for a referral will contain an allowance for an average number of non-attenders. In the early stages of the scheme it is unlikely that provider units will be able to estimate the cost of non-attenders and charge for them individually.

Duration

It is advantageous for both providers and fund-holders if as many contracts as possible are arranged in advance. This will mean that fund-holders will be assured that they have the ability to treat their patients and provider units will have the security of knowing that a certain level of funding will be available to them from this source.

The duration of the contracts will vary according to the type; it will be most critical with block contracts. Providers will need reasonable security before deploying the necessary resources – purchasers will want to ensure continuity of care. Fund-holders' contracts operate on an annual basis.

Quality

The contractual process should be regarded as a means of improving the quality of services provided. For 1991/92 if referral and activity patterns are retained at current levels, it may in practice be the only substantive change seen.

Purchasers will want to examine both clinical and non-clinical aspects in specifying and letting contracts. In particular they will want to be reassured that the contract will seek to guarantee:

- the appropriateness of treatment and care
- an optimum clinical outcome
- a minimum chance of complications and similar preventable events
- an appropriate environment
- convenience for patients/relatives/friends
- patient involvement, if wished.

For many aspects of care, indicators will need to be used as quality monitoring devices.

Consumer satisfaction

Because of the White Paper's emphasis on the patient as consumer, consumer satisfaction is a good starting point. A fund-holder might ask to see the following.

1. The information given to patients about the organization of the hospital and what they can expect to happen to them during their stay. What information are they given about their condition and treatment?
2. Patient satisfaction survey data.
3. Details of how complaints are handled.
4. Data on waiting lists and waiting times.

Clinical care

These can either be:

- general measures of clinical care (readmission rates, infection rates etc), or
- indicators relevant to particular conditions or treatments.

Either sort of indicator can deal with structure, process or outcome. For example taking some general indicators:

Structure indicators

- staffing data – ratio of qualified to unqualified staff
- number of training schemes with full accreditation.

Process indicators

- percentage of first out-patient visits where a patient is seen by a consultant
- waiting times to out-patient appointment and to treatment
- percentage of day.case work undertaken by specialty.

Outcome indicators

- infection rates
- readmission rates by specialty
- complication rates, anaesthetic reactions, adverse drug reactions
- length of stay as a proxy measure for complication rates
- death as a percentage of discharges.

This is getting to be very complex information to monitor. The purchaser would need to know what sort of answers are acceptable.

For some indicators, for example length of stay, there are national averages by specialty but for others information would need to be collected to give comparisons or the purchasers would need to make their own judgment about acceptability. The fund-holder may be better off saying, 'we expect you to have good infection control procedures and your own mechanism for monitoring infection rates', rather than asking for detailed statistics.

In future it is likely that clinical indicator development will be less concerned with these general measures than with specific diseases and conditions. What consumers, and therefore a purchaser acting on their behalf, wants to know is the relative risk associated with a particular procedure and the outcome statistics of the facility where the procedure is to be performed.

Contracts also open the door to specifying the appropriateness of the treatment for a particular set of clinical indications. An initial step in this direction would be for purchasers to decide at what point in the spread of a new technique or procedure they are willing to purchase it for their population.

Organizational standards

There are many activities which go on in a hospital which help in the overall aim of ensuring high quality patient care. These will also need to be addressed, for example:

- health and safety regulations and good practice – how far does the hospital comply? For example, when did the environmental health officer last inspect the kitchens?
- how are the internal and external cleaning contractors monitored?
- is there evidence that the hospital has an effective infection control policy?
- are drug formularies in use?

- what quality assurance methods are in operation? Is medical audit established across all specialties and working satisfactorily?

Some of the main issues to be addressed in defining quality for inclusion in contracts are:

- will the purchaser or the provider drive the process?
- different customers/clients may have different preferences
- the level of detail to be specified in contracts
- the monitoring mechanisms to be established
- the cost of improving and monitoring quality.

As mentioned above, related to this are the different approaches to the relationship between the purchaser and the provider in quality specification. These can range through:

- full specification for every service and detailed monitoring arrangements
- a requirement that systems eg medical audit are in place in the provider units
- exception reporting
- mutual trust.

Most quality measures will fall into five broad categories:

- guarantees of adhering to legal requirements. National codes of practice or explicit standards
- the provision of systems, such as medical audit, intended to assure quality
- setting of specific standards or key indicators of performance on matters of general concern or specific local interest
- setting specific clinical outcome requirements both applicable and related to specific clinical conditions

- 'common law' – a general assumption of standards which could reasonably be expected from a hospital operating in a UK medical environment.

Quality measures should only be introduced into contracts if they:

- are significant
- can be readily measured
- improvements can be made
- have relevance to the patient
- do not trigger excessive expectations, and
- are under the providers' control.

Access to premises and data

Contracts should provide for purchasers to be able to pay both announced and unannounced visits to the health care units specified in contracts to check whether standards as promised in the specification are being provided. The purchaser should also have access to any data which is specified in the contract as being necessary to its monitoring.

Pricing

Suppliers have worked out the prices they propose to charge for their services and this will form a major part of their supply proposals.

Pricing for fund-holders' contracts follow three basic principles:

- prices should be based on costs
- costs should generally be full costs
- there should be no planned cross-subsidization.

The stated price or prices within a contract will obviously reflect the type of contract and quantity involved. If a contract is for a particular speciality it may be necessary to negotiate prices which reflect different types of workload within that speciality. The factors the provider will assess in deriving a price include:

- quantity (number and severity)
- quality
- costs (fixed and variable)
- competitive price level.

In setting prices the provider will give consideration to both current costs and to prospective increases during the contract period. Some DHA contracts may include clauses for price variation in response to unpredicted events. This is considered to be inappropriate for fund-holder's contracts because:

- they will have much less scope than DHAs to hold sums in reserve for such eventualities
- fund-holders' contracts will have the maximum duration of one year so there will be much less uncertainty for provider units.

Prices of fund-holders' contracts will therefore be fixed.

The issues the purchaser will need to address include:

- is the price affordable?
- is it a fair price for the service in question?
- is there scope for the supplier to improve on the price offered?
- what modification of the service specification would bring the price to an affordable level?

In addressing these questions the first aim of the fund-holder, where prices were not affordable or seemed not to be fair, would be to secure a change in price. They would be helped in this if they had 'benchmarks' of costs for different types of treatment.

Disputes

The aim of the new contractual basis for health care is to maximize the health care provision resulting from spending taxpayers' money. Contracting should maximize the total quantity and quality of service and no District, doctor or hospital will be allowed to exploit short-term competitive advantages. Purchaser or provider cartels, or abuse of a monopoly position will not be permitted.

The legal aspects of fund holding are addressed fully in Chapter 9.

Monitoring

Both the purchaser and provider need to agree a monitoring mechanism which will identify any variations from the agreed contract. This mechanism will benefit from a small number of key indicators which reveal that the contract is on course.

Conclusion

Contracts, together with the separation of the purchaser/provider functions and the emphasis on devolution, provide an important vehicle through which the patient has priority and quality and efficiency improvements are a primary goal.

There are some important points to be remembered in the new environment:

- establishing an NHS contract should be not be approached as a legalistic or adversarial exercise but as an opportunity to discuss and agree how improvements to patient care can be secured

- medical, nursing and other professional staff should be involved in looking at existing service strengths and weaknesses, and agreeing service specifications and standards for inclusion in contracts
- the needs and views of patients should increasingly influence the delivery of the service at all levels
- the contracting process should be viewed as developmental and the degree and speed of change can only be determined locally.

9 The Legal Aspects of Fund Holding

Tim Young

This chapter deals with the requirements for recognition as a fund-holding practice and some of the legal issues to be addressed in connection with fund-holding status.

Eligibility

Any one or more medical practitioners providing general medical services in accordance with arrangements under Section 29 of the National Health Services Act 1977 (the '1977 Act') may apply to the relevant Regional Health Authority for recognition as a fund-holding practice – Section 14(1) National Health Service and Community Care Act 1990 (the '1990 Act'). A medical practitioner who becomes a fund-holder remains a general practitioner within the NHS. The National Health Service (General Medical and Pharmaceutical Services) Regulations 1974 continue to apply to him.

The relevant RHA for these purposes is the one in whose Region lies the whole or the greater part of the practice's Family Health Services Authority's locality. The relevant FHSA is the one on whose medical list the members of the practice are included. Where the medical practitioners wishing to make the application are on different FHSA's lists, then the relevant FHSA is determined as if they were all practising in a single partnership and will be the one in whose locality resides the largest number of patients on the practice list.

In the case of Scotland, application is made to the relevant Health Board and in Wales to the Secretary of State.

It is not necessary for the medical practitioners making an application to be in partnership. Practices can group together for this purpose and smaller practices may need to do so to meet the eligibility requirements.

The White Paper *Working for Patients* proposed that participation in the scheme would be limited to practices with lists of at least 11,000 patients, which is twice the national average. That figure has subsequently been reduced to 9,000. The Secretary of State has expressed sympathy with the request that practices with fewer than 9,000 patients be allowed to join the scheme and that it be extended to cover a wider range of services. These possibilities for the development of GP fund holding are being explored through a series of demonstration projects.

Conditions for recognition

The relevant RHA cannot grant recognition, in cases of practices grouping together, where the prospective fund-holding practice includes both a member who practises in partnership and the total number of patients on the lists of patients of that partnership exceeds 9,000, and a member who practises in another such partnership. The intention is presumably to avoid the creation of excessively large individual fund-holding practices. Subject to that qualification, the RHA is required to grant recognition where it is satisfied that all of the following conditions are fulfilled.

1. On the date of application there will be a total of at least 9,000 patients on the lists of patients of members of the practice, or it is likely that there will be a total of at least 9,000 patients on those lists on the date on which any recognition is to take effect.

2. Where some or all of the members of the practice are practising in partnership, the application is made (whether or not with some other persons, eg on a grouping of practices) by all the members of the partnership. Individual members of the partner-

ship will not therefore be able to opt out of joining the scheme and still remain partners.

3. The practice is capable of managing an allotted sum effectively and efficiently and, in particular, it possesses, or has access to, equipment and expertise such as computers and ancillary equipment and expertise necessary to enable it to manage an allotted sum effectively and efficiently. The phrase 'effectively and efficiently' introduces value for money concepts. Is the allotted sum being used to meet the objectives for which it is provided and in a cost-effective manner? The Department of Health has agreed to the full reimbursement of the costs of GP fund-holding computer software, maintenance and associated training, where the costs are reasonable and the software package is developed specifically for and, can be used only for, the management of practice funds. Assistance is also available for the purchasing and upgrading of hardware.

4. Where the members of the practice are not partners in a single partnership, the members of the practice have entered into an agreement approved by the RHA which provides that any act of a member of the practice with respect to the allotted sum binds the other members of the practice. Where practices group together for the purposes of applying for GP fund-holding practice status, it will be important that they have clear understandings, in written form, as to how decisions in the fund-holding practice are to be made, its management and administration.

Timing of application

Recognition as a fund-holding practice takes effect from 1 April and application for recognition has to be made by 1 April in the preceding year.

Determination of application

The RHA is required to send to each member of the practice notice of and reasons for its decision. Where it has refused recognition, it must inform each member of the practice of the right to appeal to the Secretary of State against that refusal.

Appeals to the Secretary of State

Any appeal to the Secretary of State where recognition has been refused must be made within one month, beginning on the date on which notice of the RHA's decision was sent to the members of the practice. The presumption is likely to be that the date of the RHA's notice is the date that it was sent, but it would be sensible to keep a note of the date the notice is received and the postmark on the letter, in case any dispute subsequently arises as to when time began to run for the purposes of calculating the period in which the appeal has to be made.

The notice of appeal must be signed by all the members of the practice and contain a concise statement of the grounds of appeal on which the practice relies. The Secretary of State will send a copy of the notice to the RHA.

The Secretary of State can decide the appeal on the basis of written representations, if he considers it can properly be determined without an oral hearing. If he decides that an oral hearing is required, then he will appoint one or more persons to hear the appeal. He will take into consideration the report of the person, or persons, hearing the appeal when making his decision. In effect, he reconsiders the application on the basis of the facts brought out in the appeal process.

Conditions for continuing recognition

Having achieved fund-holding status, the practice has to fulfil various conditions if it is to continue to be entitled to recognition. Apart from continuing compliance with the conditions for original recognition, there are conditions relating to the maintenance of a fund-holding account for receipt of the allotted sum and the provision of information and accounts to the relevant FHSA. There are restrictions on demanding or accepting payments (including payments in kind) for treatment of patients except in certain specified circumstances.

The goods and services which may be purchased with the allotted sum, other than general medical services, are specified in a list approved by the Secretary of State. It is a condition for continuing recognition as a fund-holding practice that none of these goods or services shall be purchased for a patient of a member of the practice 'from any person or body with which any member of the practice has a particular connection', unless:

- the relevant RHA has consented in writing to the purchase of those goods or services from that person or body, or
- it is impracticable, having regard to the condition of the patient, to obtain the consent and no alternative is available, or
- the body is a health service body other than a fund-holding practice.

The relevant regulations, the National Health Service (Fund-holding Practices) (General) Regulations 1991 ('the Regulations') define in some detail when a member of a fund-holding practice shall be treated as having 'a particular connection' with a body (as opposed to a person). Such a connection exists if a member:

- is a director of, or is in the employment of, the body; or
- is a partner of, or is in the employment of, or is a close relative of, a person who is a director of the body; or

- where the body is a fund-holding practice, he is a close relative of a member of the practice; or
- is a close relative of a person in the employment of the body; or
- has a beneficial interest in the securities of the body (eg where shares in a company are held in his name or by his nominee).

The Regulations also provide that a member of the fund-holding practice shall be treated as having 'a particular interest in a person' if he is a close relative of, or is a partner of, or is in the employment of the person. As the phrase 'a particular interest in a person' is not used elsewhere in the Regulations, this may be an error of drafting and what was intended was to refer to a person (as opposed to a body) with which the member has 'a particular connection'. It would probably be so construed in practice by a Court. 'Close relative' for these purposes means a husband, wife, brother, sister, father, mother, son or daughter.

Attempts, therefore, to set up a separate company or partnership, in which a member of the fund-holding practice has a direct or indirect interest, to supply to the practice goods or services which can be paid out of the allotted sum are likely to fall foul of these provisions and to endanger the continuing recognition of the fund-holding practice of which he is a member, unless the relevant consents are obtained.

Additions to existing fund-holding practices

If a medical practitioner wishes to join an existing fund-holding practice, then he and the members of the existing fund-holding practice would have to make a new application to the relevant RHA for recognition. However, this requirement does not apply to a medical practitioner who becomes a partner of a member of the fund-holding practice as a result of a grant of a successful application by him to an FHSA under Section 30(1) of the 1977 Act to be included in the list of names of medical practitioners undertaking to provide general medical services in the FHSA's locality. He will be treated as a member of the fund-holding practice, although he did not join in the original application.

Withdrawal of a member of a fund-holding practice

A member of a fund-holding practice can withdraw from a practice and its recognition will not be affected by the withdrawal, although it might be if the effect of the withdrawal was to reduce the number of patients of the practice below 9,000. However, a member who is a partner of another member of the practice cannot withdraw, unless he ceases to be the partner of the member remaining in the practice.

Death of a member

The death of a member of the fund-holding practice will not of itself affect its recognition.

Renunciation of recognition

A majority of members of a fund-holding practice may renounce recognition by sending notice of their intention to do so to the relevant RHA. What is meant by a majority is not defined in the Regulations. Presumably, it is a majority of individual members of the practice, rather than of partnerships, where a fund-holding practice consists of a grouping of practices. Where there is such a group, this question of renunciation of recognition is another matter which should be addressed when the group are considering the ground rules to apply to relations between themselves.

The notice of renunciation has to be in writing and signed by a majority of the members of the fund-holding practice. It must be sent at least one month before 31 March following the sending of the notice and be expressed to expire on 31 March. It will be important, therefore, to be conscious of the deadline for giving the notice, otherwise the practice may have to continue for another year. Adequate time should be allowed to prepare the notice, as it has to be accompanied by a statement including information relating to:

- the NHS contracts into which members of the practice have entered
- the amount standing in the fund-holding account (presumably at the date the notice is given)
- the amount standing in the fund-holding account which may be applied by way of savings from the allotted sum
- the liabilities of the members of the practice.

As from 31 March stated in the notice, the practice will cease to be a recognized fund-holding practice. It will, however, be required to fulfil certain conditions regarding the fund-holding account and the allotted sum until the RHA is satisfied that all the liabilities of the former fund-holding practice have been discharged.

Once the RHA is satisfied that all the liabilities have been discharged, it will give notice to that effect to each member of the former fund-holding practice. If, after renunciation, no part of the allotted sum remains in the fund-holding account, but the liabilities of the practice have not been discharged, then the RHA can transfer all the rights and liabilities of the practice to itself. Where the liabilities have been discharged and there are still monies in the fund-holding account, then the practice may apply that sum only for the prescribed purposes to which savings from the allotted sum can be put, ie broadly for the purpose of providing more and better service for patients by the purchase of materials or equipment and the improvement of premises.

Removal of recognition

The discretion to remove recognition is given to the relevant RHA in two situations.

1. Where, by 28 February in any year, the RHA has notified the members of the practice of the amount of the allotted sum for the financial year beginning on 1 April and the members of the practice have not within one month from the date that the RHA's notice is sent, notified it that they accept that amount as their allotted sum. The Regulations seem to contemplate that the notice removing recognition will take effect on 1 April succeeding it, as the provisions on procedure for removing recognition state that the removal has effect from 1 April following the sending of the notice. If the RHA does not notify the allotted sum until the last possible minute, ie 28 February, and then has to wait for one month, it will have virtually no time to send the notice removing recognition from 1 April. There is a right of appeal to the Secretary of State against removal of recognition on these grounds.

2. The RHA may also remove recognition if any of the conditions for continuing recognition is no longer fulfilled in relation to the practice. This notice can be given at any time, but removal of recognition has to take effect at least three months from the date of the notice. There are detailed provisions in the Regulations regarding the making of representations to the RHA, orally or in writing, by members of the practice in response to such a notice and of the right of appeal to the Secretary of State.

Removal of recognition with immediate effect

In the circumstances set out in the previous paragraph, the RHA has the discretion whether or not to remove recognition. It is, however, required to remove recognition with immediate effect where it appears to the RHA that it is necessary either:

- in the interests of patients of members of the practice; or
- for the purposes of ensuring proper management of the allotted sum.

There is a right of appeal to the Secretary of State.

Consequences of removal

On the day that removal of recognition takes effect, all the rights and liabilities of the fund-holding practice transfer to the RHA. It may also deal with the allotted sum as though it was the fund-holding practice, except for any savings from the allotted sum made by the practice which the RHA shall apply for such of the purposes permitted by the Regulations as the former fund-holding practice may require.

Allotted sum – authorized purposes

There are detailed provisions in the Regulations dealing with the purposes for which the allotted sum may be applied. The relevant FHSA has responsibility for day-to-day monitoring of fund expenditure and hospital activity statistics and will monitor fund-holders' expenditure on behalf of the relevant RHA.

NHS contracts

Fund-holders will place contracts with provider units, be they a directly managed unit (DMU) or NHS trust. In the case of a DMU, as it has no separate legal personality, the contract will be with its District Health Authority (DHA).

The 1990 Act creates a new species of contract for which there are no obvious parallells in English law, called an NHS contract. Section 4 of the Act defines an NHS contract as meaning *'an arrangement under which one health service body ('the acquirer') arranges for the provision to it by another health service body ('the provider') of goods or services which it reasonably requires for the purposes of its functions'*. 'Health service body' for this purpose includes health authorities, FHSAs, NHS trusts and fund-holding practices.

It is important to appreciate that it is the intention that NHS contracts should not be contracts in the proper legal sense, even if they look like any other commercial contract. Section 4(3) of the 1990 Act provides that if an NHS contract were to be a contract in law, it shall not be regarded for any purpose as giving rise to contractual rights or liabilities. The justification for this provision is that as NHS contracts are agreements between publicly funded bodies, Ministers do not consider it right for disputes between health service bodies to be susceptible to litigation in the Courts. Section 4(3) attempts to preclude this possibility. Whether that attempt has been successful is a matter for debate and the Courts will look closely at provisions ousting their jurisdiction. For example, any determination by the Secretary of State of a dispute about an NHS contract referred to him is likely to be capable of being subject to judicial review.

Resolution of disputes

As the intention is that recourse cannot be had to the Courts, either party can refer a dispute in connection with an NHS contract to the Secretary of State for determination. The 1990 Act also introduces another novel concept, which is the procedure for resolving pre-contractual disputes. A party to a proposed NHS contract can refer the terms of that proposed contract to the Secretary of State for determination. It has to demonstrate that the terms proposed in the negotiations by the other party are unfair, because the other party is seeking to take advantage of its position as the only, or the only practicable provider, or by reason of any other unequal bargaining position. Or where terms cannot be agreed for any other reason arising out of the relative bargaining position of the prospective parties. An example of where an unequal bargaining position might be regarded as existing would be if a purchaser threatened to stop purchasing services from the provider, or a provider threatened to cease supplying them to the purchaser, if its terms were not agreed, where there was no alternative practical provider or purchaser. Guidance from the NHS Management Executive on the subject of resolving disputes places much emphasis on the parties endeavouring to resolve contractual disputes locally and that the formal disputes procedure is really a matter of last resort.

In the case of pre-contractual disputes, the parties are expected to seek the assistance of their Regional General Manager(s) as conciliator(s). The function of a conciliator is to try and bring the parties together to reach an amicable compromise and normally he would not be expected to have powers of decision – unlike an arbitrator.

Referral of dispute to Secretary of State

Where a pre-contractual dispute or a dispute about an existing NHS contract has been referred to the Secretary of State, the intention is that he will normally appoint an independent adjudicator to act on his behalf. The proposal is that the adjudicators will be drawn from a panel composed of senior NHS managers nominated by each Region. Those managers will be employees of the Region, the DHA or an NHS trust.

The person appointed as adjudicator can invite the parties to make oral in addition to written observations and can also consult experts. There are time limits set out in the National Health Service Contracts (Dispute Resolution) Regulations 1991 for the various stages in the dispute resolution procedure, it being the intention that disputes be settled without delay.

Decisions by adjudicators are binding on both parties and wide powers are given by the 1990 Act to the Secretary of State, or the adjudicator appointed by him, including the power to vary the terms of the NHS contract, or bring it to an end. In the case of pre-contractual disputes he may specify terms to be included in the proposed NHS contract and may direct that it be proceeded with. In both situations, therefore, there are powers to impose a contract on an unwilling party.

Contractual arbitration

Parties to an NHS contract are encouraged to include provisions in their contract for agreed arbitration if a party believes that the contract has been broken, including specifying the arbitrator in the contract and the terms on which arbitration may take place. The relevant Guidelines suggest that the arbitrator should usually be their Regional General Manager. However, the inclusion of an arbitration clause in the contract does not preclude a party from invoking the statutory disputes resolution procedure.

The Guidelines also indicate that the presumption in determining a dispute under the statutory procedure is likely to be that the outcome will give effect to the agreement which was originally reached, rather than a new agreement which the parties should have reached. It is therefore important that the contract is as clear as possible from the outset. In the case of a contract enforceable in law, which an NHS contract is not, a Court or an arbitrator looks at the express terms of the contract, but other terms may be implied by law, eg that a person who supplies services will carry them out with reasonable care and skill. Also, in the case of a legal contract there are statutory restrictions on the use of certain clauses, such as exemption clauses. As NHS contracts are not to be regarded as contracts enforceable by law, it would seem to follow that these implied terms or statutory restrictions will not apply and the adjudicator will have to rely solely on the express terms of the contract.

Contracts with the private sector

Although contracts with other health service bodies are not legally enforceable, those with the private sector will be enforceable. The form of an NHS contract may not be appropriate when a fund-holding practice is contracting with the private sector for the provision of services.

Conclusions

In the checklist of items to be considered when applying for, or considering applying for, fund-holding status, should be a review of agreements. The review should cover both existing agreements and what new agreements may be needed if fund-holding status is obtained.

Partnership agreement

The existing partnership agreement should be reviewed to see what changes may be needed to accommodate the new fund-holding status. For example:

- is there an obligation on partners not to withdraw from the medical list?
- are all the partners treated as principals in the practice?
- what assets owned by the individual partners will be available to the fund-holding practice?
- does an application for fund-holding status require the unanimous consent of partners – certainly all will have to sign the application
- does the decision to renounce recognition as a fund-holding practice require the unanimous consent of the partners, although notice of renunciation to the RHA only needs to be signed by a majority of the members of the practice?

- what happens if a partner wishes to withdraw as a member of the fund-holding practice, given that in those circumstances he cannot remain a partner? Do the provisions for purchase of the share of the outgoing partner need to be reviewed? Would the valuation of that share take into account any savings from the allotted sum available to the practice?
- how much notice does a partner have to give of his wish to withdraw from the fund-holding practice?
- are any restrictive covenants on outgoing partners adequate to cover the situation of a withdrawal by a member from a fund-holding practice, or, indeed enforceable in those circumstances?

Grouping of practices

Where a group of separate practices wishes to make an application for fund-holding status, they should certainly consider entering into a written agreement between themselves, dealing with points similar to those which would be covered by a partnership agreement. In particular, thought should be given to the limits of authority of individual members of the fund-holding practice. It will be recalled that a condition of recognition by the RHA is that the members of the practice have entered into an agreement which provides that any act of a member with respect to the allotted sum binds the other members. If the fund-holding practice is to employ additional staff or ancillary services, how are these salaries and costs to be split between members? How are payments out of the allotted sum to be applied between the different practices making up the fund-holding practice?

Employment contracts

The opportunity should be taken to review employment contracts and consider what new employment contracts may be needed for staff who will be employed in the fund-holding practice.

NHS contracts

Once fund-holding status is obtained, then the practice will have to enter into NHS contracts with its providers. The form of those contracts may initially be dictated by the provider, but the fund-holding practice should consider what provisions it expects to see in the contracts and seek additions or amendments where appropriate. There may, for example, be room for fund-holders to negotiate on matters such as:

- waiting times
- level of staff treating patients
- timescale within which out-patients should be seen
- format for referral letters.

No doubt account will also be taken of the Patient's Charter.

Agreements with private sector

If the fund-holding practice is to purchase services from the private sector, then it will need to consider the form of contract, which will be legally enforceable.

10 Information Technology: Implications for Fund-holders

Nicola Amery

Introduction

Recent months have proved that the fund-holding initiative will make substantial and varied demands on all members of the health care team, not least those within general practice. These demands stem not only from the newness of the scheme, with its own terminology and disciplines, but also from the need to introduce appropriate management and administrative systems to cope with the volume of data being recorded and processed.

The consequent impact of information technology must not be underestimated, yet a clear sense of perspective must also be maintained about the limitations of computer systems and their true role within fund holding. This chapter attempts to clarify that role and to identify some of the issues involved in the implementation of fund-holding systems within general practice.

The Department of Health specification

Much has been made of the 'strictness' of the computer software specification produced by Touche Ross on behalf of the Department. It is, therefore, worth shedding some light on this area, if only to dispel some of the mystery which appears to surround it. The Requirements Specification is a document of over 130 pages, containing details of functionality, data structures, coding and validation, security controls and audit trails.

From a functional point of view, it is a generic specification. This means that the variations which are visible between software packages, are in most cases, determined by operating environments and the overall approach of the particular system suppliers. Most, if not all, the major suppliers have been subjected to the rigours of conformance test procedures, which were designed to ensure that the systems adhered to the functional requirements of the specification. There are, however, areas which are open to interpretation and it might prove an interesting exercise to re-run the conformance tests in the light of the various enhancements made to each software package.

The basic functions revolve around certain accounting procedures within a series of ledgers.

1. The financial (nominal) ledger is at the core of the system and records transactions for the following:

   - income (budgets) for hospital services, prescribing, staff etc
   - expenditure during the year (FIEA)
   - savings allocations
   - balance sheet (double-entry bookkeeping method) for current assets, liabilities, GP current account, FHSA account
   - cash payments (F1 account).

2. The referrals ledger is used to record both accounting and clinical details of each fund-holding referral. This has given rise to varying degrees of 'integration' among systems.
3. The purchase ledger deals with the recording and payment of suppliers' invoices, although for the sake of simplicity some suppliers have incorporated this facility within the nominal ledger.

In addition to these primary accounting transactions, there is also a requirement for expenditure and cash flow forecasting, albeit in approximation which manifests itself, in most systems, in the form of a simple spreadsheet.

Finally, the vast quantities of data which are recorded in the system produce the inevitable reams of paper as a result of the statutory reporting requirements. There are 27 of these standard reports covering referrals, financial schedules and forecasting statements. The content and format of each of these reports has been defined in detail by the specification to enable easier analysis by outside bodies such as the FHSA. However simplicity and artistic design have not been borne in mind! Some further exploration of these reports would therefore be recommended during the period of systems training and implementation.

From this overview, it should be clear that the emphasis of the fund-holding software looks towards accounting rather than practice management functions, although there is much within the specification which lends itself usefully to the general management of certain aspects of fund holding. These include monitoring referral costs, referral rates, patient costs, waiting times etc. Maximum benefit however, can only be derived from sensible preparation and planning and appreciation of the fund-holding system as an integral part of the practice's information technology (IT) system.

Preparation and planning systems

In most Regions, Health Authorities have been given considerable guidance on the preparations for fund holding, although advice on computer systems was variable. Clearly, one area of emphasis in the preparatory year has been the collection of referral statistics in order to help in contract negotiations. The nature and scope of these statistics varied enormously from Region to Region and consequently different methods of collecting the data were recommended. Ideally, these data should be collected over a whole year to provide for seasonal variations and the most obvious source of such data would be a general practice computer. This may be a fund-holding system, a clinical management system, or a combination of both. The value of computer collated data, however, does depend on the nature of the data set stipulated by each Region, as well as the appropriateness of the existing computer. Perhaps the most important issue is the 'quality' of the data which has been/can be collected in the practice over an extended period of time. Any computer user will be familiar with the adage 'garbage in, garbage out', which becomes even more pertinent if the practice is to use computer-held data as the basis for financial decision making and business planning. In theory, those practices which have been recording information for the Data Research Schemes should be well disciplined in this respect.

One of the prerequisites of the fund-holding initiative is that participating practices should have 'adequate' levels of computerization. This may or may not include consulting room screens, depending on the set-up and management structures which are already in place. Yet, part of the success of fund holding lies in how well the facilities are developed to cope with the extra commitment imposed by the scheme.

As already mentioned, a considerable volume of paperwork is generated through the daily processes of referrals and invoices as well as the monthly and ad hoc reports. Experience has shown that the ideal team to administer all aspects of fund holding should include, as well as the business/fund manager, a computer operator/s who will be responsible for generating and processing referrals. Office logistics are therefore important and the planning period should include preparation of the computer location. Thought should also be given to providing space not only for the computer but also for photocopier, fax machine, filing cabinets and so on. The fund-holding computer will provide the focal point for the fund-holding processes, but information will have to be gleaned from a number of areas both from within the practice as well as outside bodies. The data flow might best be demonstrated as in Figure 10.1.

Much of the clinical data which initiates the fund-holding referral should be collected by the clinical management computer. If it is not, then provision must be made for manual recording and collection.

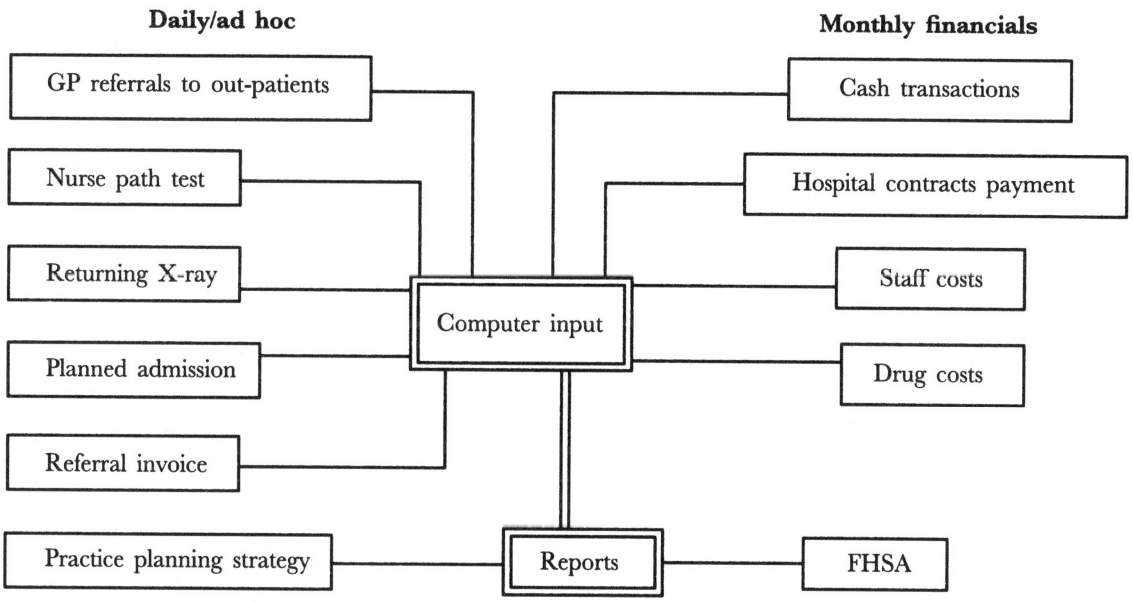

Figure 10.1: Data flow.

Installation and implementation

If all the computer systems conform to the Department of Health specification which one should the practice choose?

In most cases the practice will have already been through the decision making process of selecting a practice management system and while the same rules should apply to fund-holding systems, there are additional considerations which should not be ignored. Computers for fund holding cannot and should not be viewed in isolation, even if in the short term their function appears narrow. Long term commitment of the supplier to fund-holding development is as important as commitment to the clinical management system. Use of computers in general practice has expanded beyond all recognition and there seems no respite from the ever growing demands for increased functionality and, perhaps more importantly, increased integration.

The definitions and perceptions of 'integration' are numerous and wide-ranging, but at a basic level, the direction should be towards one-step data entry. The most obvious benefit is reduced keyboard time as well as a better method for maintaining accurate and validated data. This is true of all aspects of GP systems, but complete valid data is at the very heart of the fund-holding initiative. The underlying message, therefore, is to consider the long term implications of a certain system and its supplier.

Although almost all suppliers profess the simplicity of their software, it would be unwise not to take training seriously. A good understanding of some basic and relevant accounting principles, including double-entry bookkeeping, should be fundamental to this training period. Most suppliers provide comprehensive training programmes on their own systems and how to implement those systems most effectively within the context of fund holding. However, additional advice on the wider implications and issues of fund holding will always by useful. This type of broader training should include the mechanisms of data collection within the practice, the preparation of standard data eg hospital references and contracts as well as internal procedures for data validation. These generic courses are provided in certain areas by FHSAs and Regions as well as some system suppliers and they are worth investigating.

Conclusion

Perhaps the most extraordinary aspect of fund holding to date is the enormous variation between Regions in the approach to computerization and the consequent policies and recommendations which have been put in place. This may be because of the high profile nature of the initiative and the computer reimbursement schemes have undoubtedly exacerbated this. However, why rush to install a fund-holding computer? Apart from the obvious political and monetary influences, there is a clear need for practices to implement additional management systems and the computer is one of these. The successful introduction of any new system and particularly a computer system, requires discipline, concentration and, more than anything else, a lot of time.

Fund holding is still in its infancy and while the learning curve is very steep it is often underestimated. The controls which are inherent in the software application will be new to most practices, yet by their very nature will assist in the overall implementation of fund holding. The sooner the system is in place, the better chance practices will have to really get to grips with new procedures and management structures.

11 The Role of IT in Financial Management

David J Horrell

Introduction

A fund-holding practice holds three indicative budgets: hospital services, drug costs and staff costs. The financial performance of each of these has to be monitored together with the statistical data produced.

Drug costs are monitored on the basis of actual expenditure against budget and involve a single amount notified by PACT (Prescribing Analysis and Cost). Reimbursable staff costs are extracted from the practice payroll. The administrative burden for the practice is monitoring hospital services.

It is important to remember that the clinical activity of the practice must not be impeded so procedures must be established which do not delay consultations or clinical referral.

The Department of Health specification for fund holding computer systems was drawn up in conjunction with their advisers Touche Ross, and all data collected by the practice (both financial and statistical) must conform to the format specified. However, given such general specifications the practice may in addition require more detailed information and more flexibility. The specifications from the Department of Health should be seen as the 'skeleton' which is the standard, and the form around the skeleton is a matter of design, altered to take account of the requirements of the user.

Patient data

The data contained within age/sex registers held on computer varies greatly from practice to practice. There is often no standard format for either the information stored or the field sizes.

However, patient data for fund-holding practices is strictly specified; and it covers not only content but also specific field sizes and mandatory fields. A fund-holding patient is recognized by a unique combination of his/her NHS number and date of birth (both of which are mandatory fields).

Unlike non-fund-holding practices the absence of an NHS number cannot be ignored. The Department of Health has specified that where the NHS number is unknown a '?' symbol must be used. The surname and forename of a patient are mandatory fields as is the first line of address, town and the first section of the postcode.

Each patient record contains the code of the registered GP (known as the PPA code), prefixed by a 'G' and suffixed by a check digit. These codes together with the fund-holder and practice codes are supplied by the FHSA.

Temporary residents are coded in the same way as a registered patient but must be coded as such within the system. Therefore the same data is required but a practice has to record not only the patient's usual address (postcode is not mandatory) but also their temporary address (first section of the postcode is mandatory). A temporary patient will obviously require a '?' for the NHS number and cannot be registered with one of the practice GPs. They are therefore registered with a GP having the code of G999999.

A temporary resident must always be referred against a cost per case contract but the fund-holder does not bear the referral costs.

Referral costs and contracts

The costing of hospital services is at two levels – the first level to individual referral and the second to the patient. A patient cost is the build-up of individual referral costs and at this level the practice is only responsible for expenditure up to £5000 in any fiscal year (a fiscal year being to 31 March). Referrals will continue to be made for a patient whose actual costs have reached £5000, but anything in excess of this will be the responsibility of the DHA.

Each referral made 'picks up' the cost but this cost does not become a liability until the referral is either commenced or completed; until then the fund-holder has only a possible financial commitment. Until such time as a referral is either commenced or completed it can be cancelled by either the provider or the fund-holder.

Financial commitments fall into two categories – the present financial year and future financial years. The determining factor is the 'expected treatment date'. It is important that you are aware of how actual costs are performing against the budget and what the fund's financial commitments are for the balance of the current year and for future years.

Cost per case contracts

The definition of cost per case contracts is self-explanatory. However they are negotiated individually and are allocated a unique contract number.

Block contracts

A block contract is where a provider agrees to supply treatment for a fixed sum irrespective of the number of referrals. Most providers require the fund-holder to pay a twelfth of the annual sum monthly irrespective of the number of referrals made during that month.

The usual basis for calculation of the annual sum is by previous referral patterns, and a notional cost is set per referral. For example, treatment A has a referral pattern of 100 patients a year at a usual cost per treatment of £5 – an annual sum of £500. The notional cost is therefore set at £5. If the number of referrals falls short or exceeds the expected pattern there is no adjustment to the contract cost.

Cost and volume contracts

Cost and volume contracts are a combination of both cost per case and block contracts and can be used in two different ways.

1. The fund-holder may not wish to hold only a block contract. For example if the practice requires a block contract for treatment A up to 50 referrals and agrees an annual sum of £250 (a notional cost of £5 each) and the number of referrals actually falls short of this then the agreed sum would be payable irrespective. This would obviously guarantee the provider a fixed sum. This notional cost of £5 could be a special price because the provider is being guaranteed income, but the usual price, for a single cost per case, could be £7. The fund-holder may therefore want to negotiate that in addition to the block contract of 50 for treatment A any subsequent patients will be referred on a cost per case basis at a cost of £6. At the time of making the referral the practice would indicate whether this was a block or cost per case contract.
2. It can be used with nil volume, ie no block element. A fund-holder may wish to agree to refer a range of treatments to a provider at an agreed cost per case within a single contract on an 'as and when, and if and when' basis.

This type of contract eliminates the administrative burden of generating a cost per case contract for individual referrals.

Cancellation costs

Cancellation costs may be levied by a provider and should always be considered at the time of negotiation.

Treatment codes

The Department of Health specifies that treatments are recorded within a given coding structure which is a sub-set of OPCS4. A total of 384 codes are specified and grouped into 12 categories. However the majority of fund-holding referrals fall into two categories – out-patient services and diagnostic tests and investigations; and there is only a single code within each of these categories.

This specification is only the 'skeleton' and the overall form of the system should take into account the procedures and information required by the practice. The analysis of treatments required by practices is often determined by the contracts negotiated and by the referral statistics required (either for current performance appraisal or future contract negotiation). The Department of Health specification is not finite and the computer system used must conform to their requirements, however that should not preclude additional features being built into the design.

The preparatory year

The adage 'the earlier you start the better you will be prepared' is very apt for practices preparing for fund holding.

A practice should involve those staff members who are going to operate the computer systems and ancillary procedures early on in the preparatory year. The main concepts of fund holding are not complex, but learning about the financial and computing aspects can be confusing for staff who are not familiar with bookkeeping and accounts.

Each practice is required by the RHA to 'capture' referral statistics in the preparatory year. This information is required for the setting of the budget and for the negotiation of contracts with providers. Each RHA has its own policy for data capture, the coding to be used (which is usually more extensive than the standard fund-holding coding) and the period over which statistics are to be captured.

Choosing a computer system

In the future the Department of Health specification is bound to be amended. However you should remember that these amendments may still not provide the additional information that your practice requires; therefore you should always look at computer systems with your individual requirements in mind.

A practice has to choose which system it will use taking into account the suitability of the supplier, quality of service, training, support and the profile of the product.

You do not have to purchase a system from the supplier who supplied the basic practice system.

A GP making a referral in the consulting room is not interested in knowing which contract the referral is going to be put against and at what cost; nor whether the patient exists within the basic practice system; nor even whether all the mandatory fields required by fund holding exist. This can make the interaction between the basic practice system and the fund-holding computer system very inefficient. Inefficiency is also increased because clinically coded referrals have no direct relationship to fund-holding systems. Also, only a limited number of staff will have access to the fund-holding system.

Efficiency of operation is very important not only for actual computer operation but also the relevant practice procedures for collation of information.

In the design of systems you should take all these factors into account. There is no point in computerization just for the sake of it, particularly if maximum efficiency is to be gained.

A simple procedure for a computer, if not approached with all these factors taken into account, can create obstacles in day to day operations. For example, the closure of the months accounts can create a bottleneck. If a practice is obliged to wait for information to produce the financial reports before closing, there will be several days referrals to catch up with.

Remember that systems training and support for staff is very important if you wish to get the maximum benefit from the computer.

Conclusion

Simplicity is the key. Look at the basics of the subject and become familiar with the concepts before venturing into the intricacies of contracting and accounting.

Although fund holding is a new concept, accounting, contracting systems and allied matters have been around for years. A practice should not feel isolated with no-one to turn to.

12 Financial Management: Accounting Considerations

Laurence Slavin

The introduction of fund holding is a new challenge for medical practitioners. GPs have always been considered as businessmen (at least by their advisers and the Inland Revenue), and operated in a business environment. However, the 1990 Contract forced GPs to look more critically at the financial aspects of running their practice, and this has been taken one stage further with the introduction of fund holding.

Fund holding was initially known as budget holding. The change in the term was made mainly for political purposes, as budgets indicate a limit of funds rather than funds being led by demand. This concept is discussed later. During the rest of this chapter the term 'budgets' rather than funds is used as this is the more accurate description.

This chapter covers:

- what is meant by a budget?
- control of the budget
- the role of the accountant
- variance analysis
- the management fee.

What is meant by a budget?

It is worth highlighting the function of a budget – it combines the concepts of authority and responsibility. Thus designating someone a budget-holder for certain types of expenditure gives them the authority to incur expenditure against the budget without higher reference. Alongside the authority is the responsibility placed on the budget-holder to contain overall expenditure and to use resources effectively and efficiently. Thus a fund-holding practice will have increased freedom of action coupled with increased responsibility.

A budget is the formal outlining of objectives, and their means of attainment. Budgets require management planning, provide definite expectations and promote communication and co-ordination.

In terms of the fund-holding practice, the setting of objectives is the establishment of the drugs budget, the staffing levels and the referral patterns. The means of attainment is the negotiated budget.

Control of the budget

Control of the budget is vital to the success of the scheme. Budgetary control involves five main functions.

1. Planning: establishment of a budget team that will typically include some or all of the partners, a practice/budget manager, a data collection clerk and the practice accountant.

2. Communication: ensuring all members of the practice understand the objectives and the means to achieve them.

3. Motivation: encouraging all members of the practice to achieve the outlined objectives.

4. Comparison: comparison of actual with planned results. This is the area where accountants can play a most useful role.

5. Action: when events do not conform to plan, corrective action needs to be taken. Another area where the accountant can have a key role.

The role of the accountant

Planning

The accountant will have a considered opinion on the financial abilities of the practice through his work as the practice accountant. He will understand the general attitude of the practice towards finance, and will be able to guide the practice through areas they may find difficult to accept. The accountant will know where the practice and practice staff have weaknesses in relation to bookkeeping and accounting and will be able to predict likely problems in the staff's ability to run a fund-holding practice.

Communication and motivation

The accountant is the 'business' person most closely associated with the practice. He will be able to advise the practice on the effectiveness and importance of communication and motivation.

Comparison

The comparison of the budget to the actual results is critical to the success of the scheme. A possible overspend must be reported as soon as possible to allow the practice to either change working practises, or to approach the Regional Health Authority for additional funds. The software supplied to the practice will provide comprehensive reports indicating the progress of the budget on a monthly basis. Understanding these reports and drawing the correct conclusions is an area where the accountant should play an important role.

Action

The effectiveness of the action taken will depend on the speed and accuracy with which conclusions and reports can be prepared. The accountant should play a key role in this area.

A project team consisting of a lead partner, the fund holding/practice manager and the accountant should be set up with clear tasks and deadlines to steer fund holding in the practice. This team should meet regularly. For example, the monthly reports could be produced on the second Monday of the following month, the accountant assists in drawing conclusions on the following Wednesday, and a meeting with the partners held on the Thursday. A named individual should be placed in charge of the team to ensure its' effective operation. This will usually be the fund holding/practice manager.

Budgeting techniques

Variance analysis

A key technique in budgetary control is variance analysis. In simple terms, a variance is a variation from budget. For example:

It is budgeted that the practice will refer four hip replacement operations per month at a budgeted cost of £2,000 each. If the practice actually refers three hip operations at £2,700 each then the practice has an overall unfavourable variance of £100.

This however only provides limited information. Variance analysis can be used to provide further information. An overall variance can be further broken down between price variances and efficiency variances. The price variance explains the difference between actual unit price and budgeted price. The efficiency variance shows the difference between the units that should have been used and the units that were actually used. The formulas for calculating these variances are as follows.

Price variance

(Difference in unit price of inputs) × actual inputs used = price variance

Efficiency variance

(Difference in units used) × standard unit price = efficiency variance

Taking the example above, the price variance can be calculated as follows: £700 × three operations = £2,100 unfavourable variance.

The efficiency variance can be calculated as follows: One hip operation × £2,000 = £2,000 favourable variance.

To summarize:

Price variance (unfavourable)	(£2,100)
Efficiency variance (favourable)	£2,000
Overall variance (unfavourable)	(£100)

Therefore an overall variance of £100 that may have been ignored as being immaterial actually warrants further action when analysed further. The reason for the unfavourable price variances requires explanation and may justify an increase in the budget, the favourable efficiency variance should count towards a potential underspend.

Management fee

Some consideration should be given to the accounting treatment of the management fee of £16,500 in the preparatory year and the annual management fee of £33,500. The guidance from the GMSC is specific. The management fee should not be netted off against the expense but shown separately as income. This causes no problem for revenue related expenditure such as consultancy fees, locums or other services purchased with the management allowance, as the net effect in the profit and loss account will be nil. Where, however, the management fee is used for capital expenditure, the management fee will be shown in the profit and loss account and therefore subject to income tax in full, while the asset is shown in the balance sheet with only 25% of the cost allowed as a deduction from the profits on a reducing balance basis. For example, £10,000 of the management allowance used to purchase computer equipment will be treated as follows:

Year 1

Taxable income – management allowance	£10,000
Allowable expenditure (25% of cost)	£2,500
Taxable surplus	£7,500
Tax payable on the surplus at (say) 40%	£3,000

Year 2

Taxable income	–
Allowable expenditure (25% on written down balance)	£1,875
Deficit available for tax relief	£1,875
Tax saved on deficit at (say) 40%	£750

Year 3

Taxable income	–
Allowable expenditure (25% on written down value)	£1,406
Deficit available for tax relief	£1,406
Tax saved on deficit at (say) 40%	£562

Year 4

Taxable income	–
Allowable expenditure (25% on written down value)	£1,054
Deficit available for tax relief	£1,054
Tax saved on deficit at (say) 40%	£421

Year 5

Taxable income	–
Allowable expenditure (25% on written down value)	£791
Deficit available for tax relief	£791
Tax saved on deficit at (say) 40%	£316

Summary

Year 1 tax paid	£3,000
Year 2 tax reclaimed	(£750)
Year 3 tax reclaimed	(£562)
Year 4 tax reclaimed	(£421)
Year 5 tax reclaimed	(£316)
Tax still not reclaimed	£951

If the accounting treatment had been to net off the management allowance against the cost, the effect would have been as follows:

Year 1

Cost of computer equipment	£10,000
Less reimbursement	(£10,000)
Surplus/deficit to be taxed/tax relieved	–

No tax payable/no tax relief due.

It is therefore in the interests of the practice to net the allowance against the expenditure to which it relates. Although this may be in contravention of the directions given by the GMSC, there is a good precedent for adopting such an approach. Statements of Standard Accounting Practice (SSAPs) are issued by the accountancy bodies, as best practice to be adopted by practising accountants. SSAP4, The Accounting Treatment of Government Grants, gives the following guidance: *'If the grant (reimbursement) is revenue in nature, (ie relates to an expense charged in the profit and loss account) then the grant (reimbursement) should be included in the same period as the expenditure.*

If the grant (reimbursement) is capital in nature, then the grant can either be set against the cost of the asset, or by setting up the reimbursement as a liability, and allocating this to the profit and loss account on the basis as the asset is depreciated. Whichever of these two treatments is adopted, it should be clear that it would be incorrect to allocate the reimbursement to the profit and loss account when the asset remains in the balance sheet.'

Therefore practices should be advised it will be clearly in their interest to avoid following the directions given by the GMSC and to follow the treatment in SSAP4.

Some consideration needs to be given to the possibility of an underspend on the annual budget. In the writer's opinion, long term substantial savings are unlikely to be received, however some initial savings may be possible. Those savings can only be used in the year in which the savings are audited. This will be the year following the year in which the savings were made. For example, if a saving of £100,000 is saved in 1991/92, it will be audited and confirmed in 1992/93. It can only be used to pay for debts incurred in 1992/93. It cannot be used to pay off a loan incurred in 1991/92.

Careful planning needs to be given to the strategic direction of the practice. If a substantial underspend is forecast, then at the earliest opportunity, the practice needs to plan how to utilize this, for example, how it can be used to reduce the borrowings necessary in a cost rent scheme. The practice accountant, who by his very role will have a working overview of the practice should be able to advise on these matters.

A more difficult question is whether an underspend is taxable. As the underspend cannot be converted into cash, paying tax on a saving that may be difficult to realize would be most unwelcome.

The GP fund-holders' manual of accounts mentions that the funding for hospital services, drugs, staff expenses and other non-capital expenditure is taxable income, but the expenses to which it relates are tax deductable. Underspends are therefore taxable, but if the underspend is used to purchase further services (revenue expenditure) the expenditure is matched against the underspend netting off any effect. If the underspend is used to purchase capital expenditure the manual of accounts recommends that the income be netted off against the cost of the asset, in much the same way as the management allowance is described above. There is however a difference. The manual of accounts states on the same page that an underspend must, by definition, be a surplus of taxable income. If a surplus of taxable income is used to purchase capital expenditure, then the income is taxed immediately, and the asset will be eligible for capital allowance. The underspend cannot be described as a capital based grant (as in SSAP4 above) and therefore the practice may find themselves having to pay tax out of funds which are denied to them.

The guidance given in the manual of accounts for such problems is 'specific points should be discussed with the Tax Inspector responsible for the practice'. This would be unwise, and it should fall to the Department of Health to agree a statement of practice with the Board of Inland Revenue.

Summary

From the initial assessment of the practice's ability to manage a budget, to extrapolating information from reports, to advising on the tax position of the practice's fund, the practice accountant should have a key role to play in the fund-holding practice.

13 A Consortium Approach

Ian Walker

Since the inception of fund holding it has been clear that a consortium approach, not only to contracting, but to work related to fund holding in general, has several advantages.

Firstly, it has the advantage of increased buyer power and influence over provider units – the level of activity contracted for will 'impress' the unit management, and dealing with one 'group' rather than three or four different practices makes their management task more straightforward.

Secondly, the sharing of good practice and innovative ideas prevents each practice attempting to 'reinvent the wheel' and can speed problem solving when the same or similar problems have been encountered before.

Thirdly, and possibly the most important advantage for the fund manager is the security of having someone close at hand to offer assistance and encouragement.

There are three major areas that need to be concentrated on for success in the first year.

1. Identifying the initial allocation of funding and associated activity to preferred provider units.
2. Specifying priority quality requirements for contract negotiation.
3. Systems/information management to facilitate budget management and contract monitoring.

The initial decision on the proportion of funds to be allocated to provider units has tended to be based on recent experience with the practices' local unit. To date, where the practice has reasonable access to services and good communication with local consultants approximately 80% of total activity and funding has been committed at the negotiation table. Where access to the hospital for routine appointments and non-urgent procedures is poor and there are unacceptably long waiting times less has been committed initially.

Activity data

Critical to this allocation of funds has been the price per fund-holding item and a definite understanding by both parties involved as to what this price includes. A detailed analysis of the overall level of the budget together with the pricing structure is essential to understand the level of activity which can be bought during the financial year. A complicating factor in the activity planning for the first wave was the announcement of the inclusion of the chronic out-patient attender in addition to new referrals. A crude 'best guess' estimate is available from hospitals. Most specialties can provide an overall ratio of total follow up appointments to new referrals for GPs using the unit. This ratio can be used by the practice as a starting point for calculating total out-patient activity and cost. Ultimately the difficulties in approximating the current years total out-patient costs can be simplified if the provider unit will agree to a price per new referral which is inclusive of all follow up visits relevant to that referral plus all chronic attenders to that specialty from the practice. If this is done the practice has no 'threat' of the unknown extra costs of chronic out-patient attenders and the unit is relieved of the problem of identifying each out-patient episode and invoicing for them; they invoice per new referral only.

Contract negotiation

The second area of major work has been contract negotiation, so far, the most time consuming and frustrating. While individual practices have had very clear ideas on important quality related issues – discharge information, waiting times for out-patient appointments and in-patient admissions; many weeks of meetings with and telephone calls to, hospital units have been spent explaining the fund-holding concept and how it differs from the district purchaser/provider unit relationship.

One of the principal differences from this relationship is that fund-holding practices can be much more specific in detailing proposed activity and quality perspectives, thereby directly representing their patient population. District purchasers can only represent patients indirectly and thus need to be much more general in the specification and activity detail. Other major areas of difference are:

- fund-holding practices are much more flexible in adapting to possible alternative providers
- information requirements of the fund-holding budget monitoring system are more detailed than district purchasers, indeed the fund-holding software is probably three years in advance of the system capabilities of both providers and district purchasers.

The most effective way of forcing the pace in contract negotiations has been to detail the requirements of practices in activity, quality specification information and invoicing requirements through a fund-holding specific contract outline produced by the fund-holding practices. Although an easier option, using the contracts produced between district purchasers and providers allows for little differentiation and future flexibility and proves costly for practices later in the year, particularly in the area of detailed contract monitoring. Specific fund-holder contracts force hospital managers and consultants to respond to requirements in detail which facilitates more productive negotiations.

There have been a few cases where contracts have been agreed and it has subsequently been discovered that hospital managers have not read them fully and are now realizing the consequences. More seriously some hospital consultants have been unaware of them or of the fund-holding concept. It is very important that fund-holding GPs communicate directly with consultants they know well, as this 'understanding' filters through the hospital consultants, albeit slowly.

Without the agreement of those who deliver the service, contracts are not worth the paper they are written on!

It is important not to commit everything initially. If the provider unit is guaranteed all of a practice's funding up front in, say, a block contract there is very little incentive for them to improve services. Agreeing to commit further funding at the half year point if the unit is delivering the service as negotiated in the contract is a much better motivator for change and improvement.

Generally the author has overseen negotiated contracts which are a hybrid of cost and volume and cost per case. Indicative volumes are given but payment is based on actual provision of care and invoiced in arrears. If an agreement is reached to provide monthly payments up front, quarterly reviews are used to review future payments according to actual activity reported in the previous quarter. In this way the provider unit cannot become complacent about the contract.

Monitoring

The third area of activity is that of systems and information management to facilitate budget and contract monitoring.

The information requirements of both parties need to be specified exactly in the contracts and a detailed understanding needs to be fostered between the people operating the respective systems. Hospital information managers benefit from seeing the fund-holding software in operation and understanding why a contract number is required, what a referral number generated for each patient is and the importance of waiting list information and detailed patient activity and costs for contract and budget monitoring.

Each practice needs to establish a system to monitor the performance of the provider unit against the contract. Some sort of exception reporting system, similar in principle to the referral exception report on the fund-holding software, needs to be devised to bring the relevant facts and data to the attention of all parties concerned. The main areas of contract compliance monitoring used in the author's region are waiting times and discharge information which can be monitored by sampling rather than by reviewing all patient encounters with the hospital.

Conclusion

It is important that whoever is responsible for managing the three major areas of activity described above understands the interactions between the interested groups: GPs, provider units, district purchasers, FHSAs, RHAs and private providers, and actively communicates and balances the different expectations of each party. It is extremely important that fund-holders within each area communicate with each other to share ideas, concerns and possibly purchasing power to avoid being isolated and potentially vulnerable to a well prepared provider unit negotiating team.

Conclusion

14 The Future

David Colin-Thomé

Fund holding GPs must be regarded as having a primary care budget of which only some needs to be spent on hospital care. Fund holding must not be seen as an entity in itself but as a tool to deliver better quality and a wider range of services to our patients, in much the same way that computers in management are a tool to deliver such care.

Giving GPs a budget meets a basic management tenet which is that managerial responsibility should be devolved as far down the management line as is possible. For many fund-holders the short-term attraction of fund holding will be the ability to purchase hospital care, but in the case of my practice fund holding gave us more control to deliver our mission statement which states: *'We aim to provide the best possible care for our patients at all times by responding to their needs, providing accessible medical and anticipatory care of the highest standard and doing all we can to improve the social environment of our community.'*

We have also defined the core values of our partnership. This together with the mission statement was defined at one of our 'time-out' sessions (a technique I would recommend to any practice, especially one facing the pressure of fund holding, as it helps to make the partnership a cohesive unit). The core values of our practice are:

- our patients deserve the best
- quality is paramount and we should constantly monitor our care in our quest for excellence
- comprehensive disease control requires both preventive and curative services
- co-operation with all agencies contributing to primary care in our community is essential

- a commitment to maintain the education and full development of the whole team
- ideas should be regularly exchanged
- the practice should act as a resource for the community.

We incidentally used our core values in deciding whether the practice should hold a fund. We decided that fund holding did not clash with our core values so despite many political pressures outside the practice we decided to go forward and hold a budget.

To achieve the mission statement we defined the following range of services we as a practice should offer:

- diagnosis and management of acute and chronic conditions
- treatment of emergencies, where necessary in the patient's home, with appropriate referral to the secondary care sector
- follow-up and continuing care of chronic and recurring disease
- provision of services for rehabilitation after illness
- antenatal and postnatal care and access to contraceptive advice and provision
- accessible vaccination and immunization services
- screening for early signs of disease and paediatric surveillance
- health education advice
- co-ordinating services for the at-risk including children, the mentally ill, the bereaved, the elderly and carers in conjunction with social services
- encouraging appropriate use of care and support agencies and hospital-based services
- involvement in defining health care and social needs in the community and acting as an advocate for a better social environment.

The above list covers a core set of services primary care should deliver, and has been heavily influenced by the Royal College of General Practitioners. The final objective of defining need moves general practice towards a more expanded primary care role – more of which later.

A good general practice has to be professionally managed and the management allowance facilitates that process for fund-holders. We need to systematically define needs, plan to meet those needs and ensure those needs are met by reviewing the process systematically. Simply utilizing the management allowance to employ more and more administrative staff can lead to problems:

- General practice could be seen as a parody of the public sector, in that we employ more administrative staff than clinical care staff. This may be an appropriate use of resources but is one we should continually review to see if the balance is correct.
- We need to be lean and fit in our management structure in case such management monies are not always provided. Some of the management allowance should therefore be used to look at total quality management and resource management in the practice.
- Much of the increased administration required both in general practice and in provider units could be decreased, with consequent savings of administrative monies, by developing better IT links between the practice and provider units. By developing electronic links much of the duplication of administrative effort currently taking place in passing information between general practice fund-holders and hospitals can be reduced.

Resource management is necessary to allow total and individual patient care and its quality to be planned, delivered and costed more effectively. Case mix management information systems will allow clinicians both in hospital and in general practice and managers to utilize such information for improved medical audit. It will also give GPs information which may be useful in deciding which unit provides the most cost effective quality care – this is extremely important in setting contracts.

Total quality management involves continuous service improvement, a genuine customer focus, top down commitment and 'people' orientation in management. Fund-holders need to look at their own quality issues as well as expecting a quality service from provider units. Management consultants can address the issues of resource management and total quality management within practices.

The management allowance is there to help GPs move towards becoming a professionally managed organization. GP fund-holders need to spend some time in developing a strategic outlook for the practice. If management responsibility is to be devolved downwards then strategic management thinking has also to be cascaded downwards. If many fund-holders continue to adopt a strategic approach then we will have fulfilled the need of being a necessary short-term irritant to shake up the NHS.

GP fund-holders have two roles: purchasing and providing. Let us look at both in slightly more detail.

Purchasing

In the short-term there are grounds for decreasing the hospital referral element of fund holding. I feel that some of the more expensive in-patient procedures could be removed from the scheme such as exploration of the common bile duct and coronary artery bypass grafting. These are procedures which GPs can only influence in a small way, if at all. These procedures, once identified as being necessary for a patient, can in reality only be part of the remit of fund-holders if we decide to find a hospital that performs these operations more cheaply than the hospital originally chosen. This overt financial approach is certainly not helpful at this stage of fund holding in that it could further inflame consultant opinion. I feel the hospital referral element of the budget should only include categories of operations that GPs can influence more easily such as whether the services can be provided in-house rather than being referred. Currently one expensive procedure can undermine all the hard work that practices have put in in analysing out-patient referral patterns. Any savings from the out-patient element will be quickly swallowed by one expensive operation thereby masking the benefit of the change in the GP's behaviour.

In future the attraction of choosing which hospital we send patients to will depend on sophisticated information systems which will give us information on various types of activity including clinical care standards. We need information on case mix, consultants and clinical competencies and feedback on consumer issues such as waiting times and communications. There is an increasing need for electronic transfer of information across health authorities, provider units and GP fund-holders. General practice fund holding has certainly shaken up some of the former sterile health planning by setting standards and targets and pressurizing, where necessary, certain providers. This has already begun to influence health authorities. If, however, we move totally to capitation based funding GPs will have insufficient knowledge and skills to handle a budget; as a budget will be too small to cope with the variabilities of the very expensive patient and unanticipated demand. A capitation based system would have to be a partial capitation based approach similar in scope to the present system. All GP fund-holders need to be separate from health authorities to introduce an element of competition into purchasing. The way forward is to accept that large consortia health authorities may be necessary to share scarce public health skills in analysis, epidemiology and health care needs assessment, using these skills to set up appropriate contracts.

It could be argued that as the years develop, the strategic view of locality purchasing could well be within the remit of GP fund-holders. I would favour an intimate approach where locality purchasing will include GPs who have knowledge of hospital referral patterns for the more common conditions will help to set contracts for health authority staff, for social care purchasing and, where necessary, extend primary care purchasing into the use of local leisure and amenity services. This approach could also have an influence on utilizing youth centres and schools for health promotion and contraceptive issues. But how can locality purchasing be developed?

In our practice we have a public health nurse attached to us on a two year project, whose job is to define the health needs of the practice population. The aims of the project are to shift the focus from the providers of the service, to the receivers of the service, in order to ensure that the health needs of the local population are identified and met, and to explore methods by which planning an efficient delivery of effective care can best be achieved at practice level.

The objectives of the project were to provide:

- a comprehensive health profile of the practice
- an identification of the health needs of the population served
- a categorization of the needs identified
- a health strategy to cover a five year period with yearly targets
- a comprehensive stock take of the resources available to serve the population specified
- an evaluation of the role in primary care and the public health nurse's roles effect on supply and demand

The role of the public health nurse is an exciting one because we have seen it as a prototype of one particular model of health visiting. This particular approach will mean that the public health nurse/health visitor will be pivotal to the work of the primary health care team and with the aid of FHSAs and other commissioners set local contracts for, amongst others, GPs as the present nationally imposed GP contract does not take account of very local needs. A central contract could contain a set of core responsibilities for GPs and the local component would address the local issues. The public health nurse will in effect be the community physician for the local population. A role of course which some GPs may wish to take on. However the public health nurse could also be the local arm of the purchasing process, to be utilized by health authorities in setting contracts. The role of the public health nurse involves community development and would thus ensure that the local population finds some expression and involvement in setting health priorities rather than the current professional domination of needs assessment.

Providing

The really exciting challenge for GP fund holding is not the purchasing role, important though that may be. The purchasing role is important but peripheral to our responsibility of being providers of local services. Fund holding will encourage GPs to provide more services in their premises as these services can be delivered more cost effectively in primary care. Services could be provided by GPs and their staff, community unit staff or on contract by consultants, paramedics or management staff from elsewhere. This development of services in primary care will also help integrate primary and secondary care. Using an expanded team I propose the following approaches:

1. Utilizing hospital, FHSA and community unit managers to help manage general practice, thereby encouraging collaboration with such units by using management resources more effectively rather than the current duplication of management effort. Management issues which have a commonality across agencies could thus be addressed in a more efficient way. GP administration and GP clinical management will still be the perogative of the GP team alone.

2. Developing joint protocols for clinical care with consultants and paramedical staff will ensure:

- better technical care is provided in-house
- more appropriate referrals
- an integrated approach to shared care for patients
- quality guidelines are adhered to
- current best practice is adopted.

3. Developing paramedical skills such as physiotherapy to provide more services in-house and to assess referrals to hospital, hopefully reducing referrals for inappropriate cases. A gradual approach to limiting out-patient referrals will also enable hospitals to adjust to the lessening or differing demand of primary care so that the change in relationship between primary and secondary care can be handled in a controlled way. Hospitals need to be more appropriately used rather than as at present dominating health care provision. Any sudden destabilization of a hospital will damage an essential resource for the community and the GP.

4. The development of fund holding could see the re-emergence of cottage/community hospitals for low-tech, local care under the aegis of GPs and other members of the primary health care team. This may have quite important implications for future health care delivery. One could envisage an array of cottage hospitals, district general hospitals with core general services and more specialized units, such as the current regional centres on more distant sites, offering services in the rarer specialities. We will need quality feedback to ensure that quality standards are maintained. As we get more clinical care information patients may be willing to travel for treatment even in areas of poverty and low car ownership. Fund holding could subsidize a travel element for such patients if the quality or cost benefit of such distant units are clear.

5. One could envisage developing primary care such that it would become a public sector version of a health maintenance organization (HMO) providing a range of services on one or several sites, responding to local need. These units would not necessarily be GP led but GPs would provide their skills and services as an important 'part' of a greater primary care 'whole'. Primary care should meet the needs of patients. It should deliver anticipatory care in response to health needs assessment but also develop a public health approach by looking at the health needs of the community. Having a budget allows GPs to have some control in setting the priorities to meet such needs. Such a primary care approach could be GP led if GPs are skilled/trained in strategic and operational management and needs assessment.

In my description I have separated purchasing and providing, as a separation of those two entities clarifies the roles of various parts of the health service. It is a conceptual framework which has become popular in many countries. At a local level it should be viewed as a management tool to deliver better and more comprehensive services locally which is of course is the reason d'etre of fund holding.

The importance of fund holding was mentioned at the beginning of the chapter – it is a primary care budget to be utilized in meeting the needs of a local practice population. If we develop fund holding to broaden its approach to address reactive, anticipatory, public health and social care needs we can expand primary care to purchase identifiable health gain and in doing so adopt a strategic management approach to primary care. Then, whatever the hue of the government, fund holding will be preserved as fund holders will have demonstrated that primary care is truly the pivot of the NHS and deserves to remain so.

15 Where to Turn to For Help

Antoinette Pirie

Managing a complex health care delivery and financing organization, such as that proposed by the fund-holding scheme, calls for specialized personnel, management tools and techniques. The skills and expertise now called for may not be currently available within practices. The Government acknowledges that GPs may have to look to other agencies for help and a fee set at the level which recognizes the 'management and other costs associated with participation' is included in the practice allocation.

A management allowance of up to £16,500 has been made to cover costs incurred during the preparatory year. Thereafter there is an annual allowance of up to £33,500 to cover fund management costs once the practice becomes fund holding.

The allocation could go towards:

- an extra member of staff to handle budget arrangements
- training for medical and ancillary staff
- locum cover
- professional consultancy services.

As part of the initial practice review undertaken before embarking upon fund holding a skills-need and training-needs analysis should be performed.

- Are the relevant skills and systems required for successful management of fund holding in place?
- If not, can they be developed in-house and what are the associated costs and timescales?

- If they need to be bought in where can the relevant expertise/ training be found, and at what cost?

Consultancy services and training programmes are offered by a number of organizations to fill the perceived skill and knowledge gaps that the changes within general practice have uncovered.

The following is a list of organizations which offer specific services for general practice fund-holders.

Bevan Ashford Solicitors
35 Colston Avenue
Bristol BS1 4TT
Tel: 0272 230111

The firm is one of the largest practices in the country offering legal advice to health service clients via a network of offices. With a longstanding presence in this area they are well placed to advise and assist on the new issues and opportunities now facing the service.

Capita Group plc
Great West House
Great West Road
Brentford TW8 9DF
Tel: 081 560 9922

Offer general consultancy and business planning services and are keen to develop their work with fund-holders.

Centre for Health Planning and Management
University of Keele
Keele ST5 5BG
Tel: 0782 583191

The Centre is a well established multidisciplinary institute concentrating on both academic and applied health service studies. With over 40 full-time faculty staff, its portfolio of activities includes teaching, research and consultancy/advisory work.

The Centre offers a range of executive courses, workshops and seminars either on the Keele campus or on site with the client. The broad disciplines covered include:

- general management and management development
- health policy issues
- information and communications.

The Centre does not offer a specific fund-holding package and their consultants would work on an individual project basis. Areas covered by the Centre's consultants include:

- information – advising on appropriate data and information bases for planning at the small area level
- finance – designing information systems that link together finance, manpower and activity data
- primary health care – analysis of GP out-patient referrals
- medical audit – quality assurance in the primary and secondary care sectors.

Centre for Health Services Management
Leicester Business School
Leicester Polytechnic
Leicester LE1 9BH
Tel: 0533 577243 Ext. 7222

The HSM Centre has developed a package specifically aimed at fund-holders. The programme is an extended version of a workshop on financial management and business planning that was sponsored by BUPA. The one day modules cover:

- financial management
- business planning
- information needs for fund-holders.

The Centre also offers a 'tailor made' consultancy service.

Coopers Lybrand Deloitte
Plumtree Court
London EC4A 4HT
Tel: 071 583 5000

The increased budgeting and accounting/purchasing decisions being placed upon GPs by the recent changes in the NHS have led the firm to think about GPs' needs. The firm can provide the following services for GPs:

- internal audit/review
- partnership accounts audit
- systems advice/review
- small scale general consulting
- project management eg new premises
- fund raising and loan advice.

The Department for Enterprise (DTI)
Bridge Place
88–89 Eccleston Square
London SW1V 1PT
Tel: 071 627 7800

A number of fund-holding practices have turned to the DTI Enterprise Initiative for consultancy assistance. The consultancy service is available twice, for different projects, and groups with fewer than 500 employees are eligible. The DTI will pay up to two thirds of the cost of specialist help for projects lasting between five and 15 days in the following areas:

- marketing
- design
- quality
- manufacturing systems

- business planning
- financial and information systems.

The final two initiatives are of particular interest to potential fundholders. The initiatives offer a low-cost method for practices to obtain specific consultancy advice. It is particularly suitable for practices that are basically well managed and have identified weaknesses in specific areas covered by the scheme. It would not be suitable for practices needing more widespread help.

Andrew Donaldson: management, development and training
3 Tudor Gardens
Stony Stafford
Milton Keynes MK11 1HX
Tel: 0908 565020

This organization has over 25 years experience in NHS management, latterly planning district services in the Oxford Region, involving several new health and medical centres in Milton Keynes. They provide wide ranging consultancy advice including purchaser and provider contracts, medical audit and management training.

Genisyst
84 Bancroft
Hitchin SG5 1NQ
Tel: 0462 435754

Genisyst is one of the fastest growing companies in the field of GP computing.

The company is self-sufficient in all areas including development, support and electronics; and during 1992 several new and exciting products are due for release. User interest comes first not only in the supply of a high quality product, service and support but also in value for money – systems are always competitively priced.

Genisyst is committed to the development of GP computer systems and to addressing the needs of both buyers, users and NHS authorities.

Granville Sansom Personnel and Management Consultancy
The Phoenix
Napsbury Hospital
London Colney
St Albans AL2 1BN
Tel: 0727 821530

The firm has wide experience of working with general practices.

- Management support to fund-holding and non-fund-holding practices including business planning, personnel issues, staff training and internal reviews.
- PGEA approved training sessions covering business planning, marketing, contract negotiation, costing and budget setting.
- PGEA approved study tours to the Netherlands.

Work with fund-holding practices in particular includes:

- recruitment and selection of practice business managers and practice staff
- business planning support and training
- development and implementation of practice procedures and management structures
- financial analysis of practices including assessment of target performance
- liaison with the FHSA on behalf of practices.

Health Services Management Centre
University of Birmingham
Park House
40 Edgbaston Park Road
Birmingham B15 2RT
Tel: 021 414 3344

The Centre responded early to the GP funding initiative and held an initial one day conference in 1990 on some of the major issues involved. Following this a series of one and two day workshops were arranged for GPs, FHSAs, units and DHAs. The topics covered by the Centre include:

- business planning and negotiating skills for GPs
- budgetary management for GPs
- marketing hospital and community services to fund-holders
- assessing the impact of fund holding on patients
- accounting procedures for fund-holders
- quality assurance
- managing prescribing budgets.

The Centre also offers a 'tailor made' consultancy service.

The Kings Fund
14 Palace Court
London W2
and
The Kings Fund Centre
126 Albert Street
London NW1 7NF
Tel: 071 267 6111

The Kings Fund Centre provides a base for the Fund on health services development. The objective is to support innovations in the NHS and related organizations and to encourage the uptake of new ideas and good practice in healthcare. They offer a variety of seminars and courses of direct relevance to fund-holders.

Management Advisory Service
11 Royal Crescent
Cheltenham GL50 3DA
Tel: 0242 519908

MAS worked with two RHAs in the run up to fund holding. Their initial work was concerned with developing action plans for the first wave practices using fact sheets and holding workshops.

As well as helping with contracting issues such as quality measures and monitoring arrangements MAS can also provide help in the areas of data collection, training and publicity.

NHS Training and Studies Centre
Cold Bath Road
Harrogate HG2 0NF
Tel: 0423 505 681

The Centre operates from within the NHS Training Authority as an internal consultancy and development resource for the NHS and NHS Management Board. They aim to run events which are predominantly for senior staff in the service. The courses, workshops and seminars are typically tailor-made to suit a diagnosed need.

The following courses, for which PGEA accreditation has been applied for, are of relevance to fund-holders:

- medical audit programme
- managing change in general practice
- time and priorities in general practice
- an audit cycle for general practice.

Pannell Kerr Forster
Pannell House
Park Street
Guildford GU1 4HN
Tel: 0483 64646

Pannell Kerr Forster has over 50 years experience of dealing with the accountancy and financial affairs of members of the medical profession. The firm has responded to the fund-holding initiative and offers the following services to fund-holding GPs:

- the Department of Health (DoH) Helpline. In order to assist practices and managers in understanding the Manual of Accounts and to provide immediate explanation, the DoH invited Pannell Kerr Forster to set up a telephone helpline: 0483 573853

- help with the preparation of annual fund-holding accounts for the FHSA
- help with the production of practice business plans
- help with computer services in conjunction with the GP computer supplier AAH Meditel
- recruitment of specialist staff
- advice on management of savings accounts.

Price Waterhouse (Office of Healthcare Services)
Southwark Towers
London Bridge Street
London SE1 9SY
Tel: 071 939 3000

Price Waterhouse through its healthcare management consulting arm, the Office of Healthcare Services, with offices in London, Bristol and Leeds, offers a full range of assistance to GP fund-holders. Services include:

- advice on information technology from system specification to implementation
- advice on negotiating contracts with provider units including the development of quality standards
- assistance with management of practice costs
- help with the analysis and interpretation of casemix information.

In addition they are also able to offer tax advice through the tax branch of the firm.

Ramsay Brown and Partners
Ramsay House
825 High Road
Finchley
London N12 8UB
Tel: 081 445 3351

Ramsay Brown and Partners specialize in the finances of medical practitioners, and currently service more than 500 GPs, from single-handed to ten partner fund-holding practices. Both partners, Laurence Slavin and Stuart Singer, write and lecture extensively on the finances of GPs.

Peter Stanley Associates
Birch House
Startley
Nr Chippenham SN15 5HG
Tel: 0249 721172

A medium-sized consultancy practice which specializes exclusively in healthcare. Peter Stanley Associates work throughout the NHS with both purchasers and providers. The firm carries out thorough reviews of practices to identify strengths and weaknesses vis a vis fund-holding potential. Specific areas would include:

- analysis of current patient referrals and options for change
- providing a detailed 'profile of need for hospital services'
- assessing the practice business including information and accounting requirements, management and staffing structure
- roles of the partners in the management of the practice
- team building and management development
- evaluating appointment systems
- advising on purchaser specifications for hospital and community services.

Peter Stanley Associates are able to match their services to meet the specific requirements of individual practices including the provision of on-going support to provide regular 'as and when' advice.

Touche Ross
Hill House
1 Little New Street
London EC4A 3TR
Tel: 071 936 3000

Touche Ross and Spicer Oppenheim merged in 1990. The healthcare practices of the two firms were complementary – Touche Ross specialized in working at RHA and DHA level and Spicer and Oppenheim had strong links with the primary care sector.

Their consultants have worked in all parts of the health service from the Department of Health to individual purchaser and provider units, FHSAs and general practice.

Vamp Health Ltd
The Bread Factory
1a Broughton Street
London SW8 3QT
Tel: 071 498 1330

Almost one third of all fund holding practices currently use VAMP software. The firm is now well placed to help prospective fund holding practices put computer and management systems into place:

- 86 first wave installations
- multiple sites, multiple practices
- stand-alone systems or integrated with VAMP Medical
- converted patient register from non-VAMP systems
- full training and support from specialist staff.

The enormous experience gained from the first wave of fund holding has enabled VAMP to put together a comprehensive plan which goes beyond keyboard skills and computer training. Courses begin in July and broadly cover:

- planning and preparation: basic concepts, regulations and obligations of fund holding, review of the manual of accounts, basic accounting and bookkeeping, negotiating contracts, first wave experiences
- implementation part 1: contractual issues, the referral process all major processes of fund holding, software application, reports
- implementation part 2: review and revision, changes in regulations, self-sufficiency and troubleshooting.

Wilter Associates Management Consultants
Willow Court
Marsham Lane
Gerrards Cross SL9 8HD
Tel: 0753 890359

A group of six consultants with backgrounds in both the public and private sector. All the consultants have worked in the NHS either as doctors, nurses or managers. They aim to help organizations manage change whatever its basis, be it: IT, financial systems, people issues, crisis etc. The group offer a personalized service working with their clients to help them acquire skills and competencies. In all their projects they emphasize the 'soft' issues. By a combination of facilitation, creative management and organization development techniques they aim to help organizations make the cultural adjustment to the 'change catalyst' as well as designing and implementing the more obvious 'hard' solutions.

The following is a list of the other firms whose fund-holding software has passed DoH conformance testing:

AAH Meditel Ltd
Rigby Hall
Rigby Lane
Bromsgrove B60 2EW
Tel: 0527 579414

AMC Ltd
Clarendon House
The Bridal Path
Watford WD2 4AA
Tel: 0923 255740

Anglia Consultants (MTECH and AMSYS)
The Old Brewery House
The Market Square
Reepham NR10 4JJ
Tel: 0603 871999

Micro-doc
Hollowbrook House
Lydgate Lane
Sheffield S10 5SH
Tel: 04336 30497

Update Computers Ltd
19–30 Alfred Place
London WC1E 7EA
Tel: 071 580 8121

16 Common Questions Asked

Mercedes Kelly

Practices applying to join the fund-holding scheme usually have numerous questions. We have compiled a list of those most commonly asked.

Question: How much reimbursement can the practice expect if they need to upgrade their computer system and buy the fund-holding software?

Answer: Full reimbursement of costs can be made in respect of any fund-holding software package which has successfully completed conformance testing. Payments are also made for training costs associated with any of the packages.

System purchase costs: In the case of fund-holding practices, the level of reimbursement will be 75% of the actual net price of specific hardware.

Upgrading costs: Subject to the availability of funds, payment, less any deduction in respect of private income from the sale of anonymized data, will be made in respect of a proportion of the costs incurred by the practitioner, partnership or group practice in upgrading an existing computer system for the use of the practice. This includes both hardware and software costs. An existing computer system may be owned, rented or leased.

Question: What additional management expertise is needed to manage and organize the fund?

Answer: While many practice managers already in post feel confident to manage a fund, experience is showing that practices who appoint a full-time fund manager with no other practice commitments operate more successfully. In the preparatory year this person can be paid on a pro-rata, part-time basis from the management allowance. When the practice has completed the preparatory year and the management allowance is paid in full the position can then become full-time at the appropriate salary. With those practices which group together to form a consortia or co-operative, more than one management allowance will be available in the preparatory year and, therefore, it would be possible to recruit a full-time manager from the beginning of the preparatory year.

Question: How do we find out about our patients on waiting lists?

Answer: All providers will now be in a position to give a practice, by GP, the names of those patients on waiting lists either by consultant or specialty. A method of cross checking these is to put up a simple poster in the waiting room asking those patients who are on waiting lists to register at reception and cross-check.

Question: How do we find out about those patients who are now chronically ill and attend hospital out-patients?

Answer: The most effective way to locate these patients at present (as there are no records as yet for chronic attenders at out-patient clinics) is to print a clear notice asking those patients attending hospital diabetic, asthma clinics etc to advise reception. A database can be built up from this information allowing GPs to recall these patients and assess whether it is still necessary for them to be seen in the hospital-based clinic.

Question: Where do we get provider costs and who do we contact?

Answer: All providers now issue price lists directly to fund-holders or on request to prospective fund-holders. Attached to these are names and telephone numbers of the people responsible for contracts for each directorate. If this is not available then your FHSA will advise on who to contact.

Question: What happens if we overspend our budget?

Answer: The FHSA is responsible for monitoring your expenditure and the fund-holding software prints an end of each month return which enables the FHSA finance directors to project fund's expenditure. If an overspend looks like happening then the FHSA will give the necessary guidance to bring you back on course.

Question: What can we spend our savings on?

Answer: Savings cannot be identified until the end of each financial year following completion of the practice budget annual accounts. Should savings be accrued they may be spent for the benefit of your patients on:

- paying for additional staff or hospital services
- improving facilities for patients
- providing additional medical equipment.

You are not obliged to make savings and if you do you may not carry over one sum for more than four years.

Appendix: Elective Surgical Procedures Covered by the Fund-holding Scheme

Code procedure description		*OPCS 4th revision operation codes*
Ophthalmology		
A01	Operations for squint	C31 to C35
A02	Chalazion operation	C12
A03	Pterygium operation	C39.1
A04	Operations for ectropion, entropion and ptosis	C15.1 C15.2 C18
A05	Operations for glaucoma	C59 C60 C61 C62 C66.3 C66.4
A06	Operations for obstruction of the nasolacrimal duct	C25 C27
A07	Extraction of cataract with/out intra-ocular implant	C71 C72 C74 C75
A08	Corneal graft	C46
A09	Laser treatment for vascular retinopathies	C82.1
Ear, nose and throat		
B01	Myringotomy	D15.3
B02	Insertion of grommet	D15.1
B03	Mastoidectomy	D10 except D10.5

B04	Stapedectomy	D17.1 D17.2
B05	Tympanoplasty	D14
B06	Labyrinthectomy	D26.2 D26.3
B07	Septoplasty	E03.4 to E03.9
B08	Sub-mucous resection of septum	E03.1
B09	Polypectomy	E08.1
B10	Ethmoidectomy	E14.1 to E14.4
B11	Turbinectomy	E04.2
B12	Cautery of lesion of nasal mucosa	E05.1
B13	Puncture of maxillary antrum with wash-out	E13.6
B14	Drainage of maxillary sinus	E12.2 to E13.1
B15	Exploration of frontal sinus	E14.9
B16	Tonsillectomy	F34
B17	Adenoidectomy	E20.1
B18	Pharyngoscopy	E24 E25
B19	Laryngoscopy	E34 E35 E36
B20	Laryngectomy	E29
B21	Block dissection	T85.1

Thoracic

C01	Bronchoscopy with/out biopsy	E48 E49 E50 E51
C02	Biopsy/excision of lesions of lung or bronchus	E46.2 to E46.9 E47.1 E55 E59.1 to E59.3
C04	Lobectomy	E54
C05	Pneumonectomy	E54

Cardiovascular

D01	Operations for valvular or ischaemic heart diseases (excluding neonatal and infant surgery)	K25 to K35 K40 to K51

General surgery

E01	Partial thyroidectomy	B12.1 B12.2 B08.2 to B08.9
E02	Total thyroidectomy	B08.1
E03	Thyroidectomy of aberrent thyroid gland	B09.1 B09.2
E04	Operation on salivary gland and ducts	F44 to F58
E05	Operations on para-thyroid glands	B14 B16
E06	Oesophagoscopy with/out endoscopic procedures	G14 to G19
E07	Dilation of oesophagus	G18.2 G18.3 G15.2 G15.3
E08	Operation on varices of of the oesophagus	G10 G14.4 G17.4
E09	Gastrectomy partial or total	G27 G28
E10	Vagotomy with/out other operative procedure	A27 G33.1 G40.1 G40.3
E11	Endoscopy with/out endoscopic procedures	G43 G44 G45 G54 G55 G62 G64 G65 G79 G80
E12	Laparoscopy with/out biopsy	T42 T43
E13	Excision of lesion of small intestine	G50 G53.1 G59 G63.1 G70 G78
E14	Partial colectomy	H06 to H11
E15	Total colectomy	H04 H05

E16	Sigmoidoscopy with/out biopsy/polypectomy	H23 to H28
E17	Colonoscopy with/out biopsy/polypectomy	H20 H21 H22
E18	Exteriorization of bowel	H15
E19	Repair of prolapsed rectum	H35 H36 H42
E20	Operations for anal fissures and fistula	H56.4
E21	Excision of rectum	H33
E23	Pilonidal sinus	H59 H60
E24	Dilation of anal sphincter	H54
E25	Haemorrhoidectomy	H51 H52 H53
E26	Operations on the gall bladder	J18 to J26
E27	Operations on the bile ducts	J27 to J52
E28	Mastectomy	B27
E29	Excision/biopsy of breast lesion	B28 B32
E30	Repair of inguinal hernia	T19 T20 T21
E31	Repair of femoral hernia	T22 T23
E32	Repair of incisional hernia	T25 T26
E33	Varicose veins stripping/ligation	L85 L86 L87
E34	Surgical treatment of ingrowing toenail	S64 S68 S70.1
E35	Excision/biopsy of skin or subcutaneous tissue	S05 S06 S09 S10.2 S11.2 S13 S14 S15
E36	Lymph node excision/biopsy	T87

Genitourinary

F01	Cystoscopy with/out destruction of bladder lesion	M42 M44 M45 M76 M77
F02	Dilation of urethra/ urethrotomy	M76.4 M81 M58 M79 M76.3 M75
F03	Urethroplasty	M73
F04	Open repair	M73.4
F05	Prostatectomy open or TUR	M61 M65
F06	Excision of hydrocele	N11
F07	Orchidopexy	N08 N09
F08	Male sterilization	N17
F09	Circumcision	N30
F10	Varicocele	N19
F11	Removal of ureteric or renal calculus	M09 M26 M27 M28 M06.1 M23.1
F12	Lithotripsy	M14 M31
F13	Nephrectomy	M02 M03

Gynaecology

G01	Oophorectomy/salpingoophorectomy	Q22.1 Q22.3 Q23.1 Q23.2 Q23.5 Q23.6 Q24.1 Q24.3
G02	Ovarian cystectomy	Q43.2
G03	Wedge resection of ovary	Q43.1
G04	Female sterilization	Q35 Q36 Q27 Q28
G05	Patency tests of fallopian tubes	Q39.9 Q41
G06	Hysterectomy abdominal/ vaginal	Q07 Q08
G07	Myomectomy	Q09.2
G08	D and C with/out polypectomy	Q10.3

G09	Cone biopsy	Q03.1 Q03.3
G10	Colposcopy with/out biopsy of cervix	Q02 Q03.4 to Q03.9 P27.3
G11	Anterior or posterior repair	P22 P23 P24 P13.2 P13.3
G12	Vulvectomy/partial vulvectomy/vulval biopsy	P05 except P05.3 P06 P09.1
G13	Marsupialization of Bartholin's cyst/abcess	P03.2 P05.3
G14	Diagnostic laparoscopy with/out biopsy	Q39 Q50
G16	EUA	Q55.2
G17	Hysterectomy/endometrial resection	

Orthopaedics

H01	Operation on inter-vertebral discs	V29 to V35 V52
H02	Therapeutic lumbar epidural injection	A52.1
H03	Arthroplasty/revision arthoplasty of hip or knee	W37 to W42 W46 W47 W48
H04	Removal of implanted substance from bone	W35.3
H05	Upper tibial osteotomy	W12
H06	Arthroscopy with/out other intra-articular procedures	W82 to W88
H07	Intra-articular injections	W90
H08	Meniscectomy	W70 W82
H09	Corrections of hammer toe etc	W59.5
H10	Dupuytrens contracture	T52.1 T52.2
H11	Carpal tunnel decompression	A65.1

H12	Release of trigger finger	T72.3
H13	Excision of ganglion	T59 T60
H14	Aspiration/excision of bursa	T62.1 to T62.5
H15	Osteotomy for hallux valgus/rigidus	W57.1 W15

Index

CROTAL RUADH

RED LICHEN

Jenny and Ali

Beannachdan –

blessings!

Sandy

Christmas 2016

CROTAL RUADH

RED LICHEN

CRUINNEACHADH BÀRDACHD AGUS ÒRAN

COLLECTED POEMS AND SONGS

SANDAIDH NICDHÒMHNAILL JONES

acair

Tabhartas – *Dedication*

Mar chuimhneachan air m' athair agus mo mhàthair;
do John agus Katy, le taing is spèis;
agus do mhuinntir Uibhist, airson ur furain.

In memory of my father and mother;
to John and Katy with gratitude and affection;
and to the Uist community, for your welcome.

Air fhoillseachadh ann an 2016 le Acair Earranta

An Tosgan, Rathad Shìophoirt, Steòrnabhagh, Eilean Leòdhais HS1 2SD

www.acairbooks.com
info@acairbooks.com

Deilbhte agus dèanta le Acair Earranta

Dealbhachadh an teacsa agus an còmhdach le Joan Macrae-Smith air leth Acair

An dealbh-còmhdaich le Sandaidh NicDhòmhnaill

Chuidich Comhairle nan Leabhraichean am foillsichear le cosgaisean an leabhair seo.

Tha Acair a' faighinn taic bho Bhòrd na Gàidhlig.

Gheibhear clàr catalog CIP airson an leabhair seo ann an Leabharlann Bhreatainn.

Clò-bhuailte le Hussar Books, A' Phòlainn

LAGE/ISBN: 978-0-86152-401-3

Poems in this collection previously published:

'Na Fir-Chlis', Winner of Col. Eoghain Uí Néill Poetry Competition, 2014, published on Comhdhail Comórtas Filíochta website 2014
'Geaco Mascarene', Winner of Wigtown Gaelic Poetry Competition 2013, in' Southlight' 14, Autumn 2013
'Crodh-Golf Aisgernis' and 'Na Fir-Chlis', in 'New Writing', New Writers Awards 2010/2011 Sampler Collection, Scottish Book Trust, Edinburgh, 2012
'Reachd' in 'An Guth', Coisceim, Dublin 2013; and in 'Northwords Now', Issue 24, Summer 2013.

Molaidhean - *Commendations*

'Bha na h-òrain a sheall Sandaidh dhomh, ann am pòsadh fonn is facal, cho coileanta 's a dh'iarras: bha siùbhlachd deiseil anns an ruitheam, agus seirm impidheach ann am fonn nam facal. Bha e fhathast follaiseach gun robh blas, agus brìgh, na bàrdachd a' ruith tro gach oidhirp a chunnaic mi. Tha i comasach, nuair a tha e iomchaidh, air tionndaidhean annasach, uaireanan èibhinn no clisgeach a thoirt air smuaint na bàrdachd.'
'The songs Sandy showed to me were as fully-formed as could be wished in marrying tune to words: the rhythms flowed readily, and the word-cadences had a convincing ring to them. It was already clear that the idiom and meaning of poetry coursed through every piece of her writing that I read. She has a well-judged touch for adding unusual, and sometimes witty or skittish twists to the concepts in the poetry.'

Aonghas 'Dubh' MacNeacail

"Tha iongantas agus cànan an sàs ann am bàrdachd cho math ri smuain. Tha iad seo an sàs ann am pailteas san dàn 'Geaco Mascarene' a bhuannaich a' cho-fharpais. 'S e fosgladh sùla a th' ann mun gheaco bheag thrìd-shoilleir chìocrach, a chaomhnas an neach-labhairt ri linn a bhith ag ithe nan cuileagan. 'S e cuspair mì-àbhaisteach a th' ann do bhàrdachd na Gàidhlig, ach tha e a' tighinn ris a' chànan gu math, le faclan drùidhteach, uaim agus fealla-dhà a tha an dà chuid dùthchasach agus ùrail."
'Poetry is about thought certainly, but also about language and surprise. The winning entry, 'Gecko Mascarene' has these elements in abundance. It opens your eyes to the little transparent ravenous gecko that saves the speaker from being eaten by biting flies. It is an unusual subject for Gaelic, but the description is completely embedded in that language, with striking words, lovely alliteration and a very Gaelic sort of humour. It feels very fresh.'

Meg Bateman

Sna dàin as fheàrr anns a' chruinneachadh seo tha ceòl na Gàidhlig eadar gheantraighe 's ghultraighe – gun tighinn air ceòl-gàire fhèin – fighte gu h-ealanta ri sealladh farsaing air an t-saoghal thoinnte sam beò sinn.'
'In the best poems in this collection, the musicality of the Gaelic, ebbing and flowing between cheerfully animated and poignantly sad verse – though never actually laughing out loud – is ingeniously woven together with a far-reaching view of the complicated world in which we live.'

Rody Gorman

SANDAIDH NICDHÒMHNAILL JONES

Sandaidh NicDhòmhnaill Jones
Geàrr-chunntas beatha an ùghdair

Bhuannaich Sandaidh Duais Bàrdachd Gàidhlig Bhaile na h-Ùige 2013; fhuair i 'moladh sònraichte' san dearbh cho-fharpais ann an 2014 agus 2012. Bhuannaich Sandaidh Farpais Bhàrdachd na Cuairte (Comórtas Filíochta an Choirnéil Eoghain Uí Néill) ann an Èirinn sa Ghiblean 2014; chaidh an dàn fhoillseachadh ann an 'Sgrìobag na Seachdain' aig Sabhal Mòr Ostaig sa Ghiblean agus Am Pàipear ann an Uibhist sa Chèitean. Chaidh pìosan bàrdachd a sgrìobh i roimhe sin fhoillseachadh ann an 'Northwords Now' agus 'An Guth' ann an 2013.

Tha ise an-dràsta deiseil gus a' chiad chruinneachadh bàrdachd Ghàidhlig aice fhoillseachadh. Tha i air a bhith ag obair air o chionn bliadhna neo dhà, fo oideachadh bho Aonghas 'Dubh' MacNeacail, le taic bhon sgeama 'Duais Sgriobhadairean Ùra' aig Comhairle nan Leabhraichean agus Scottish Book Trust. Tha i gu sònraichte taingeil do Aonghas airson a' chuideachaidh agus comhairle, agus cuideachd taingeil airson misneachaidh a fhuair i bho Rody Gorman, Meg Bateman, Màrtainn Mac an t-Saoir, Gillebrìde Mac 'IlleMhaoil, Máire Ní Annracháin, agus càirdean eile ann an saoghal litreachais na Gàidhlig.

Thòisich Sandaidh air bàrdachd Ghàidhlig a sgrìobhadh ann an 2007, agus Gàidhlig ionnsachadh ann an 2000. Tha i gu mòr an sàs ann an ceòl Gàidhlig, mar sheinneadair agus clàrsair. Bidh i a' buannachadh dhuaisean litreachais aig Mòdan, a' gabhail a-steach Bàrdachd agus Òrain Ùra, agus cuideachd airson co-sheirmean air òrain Ghàidhlig airson chòisirean agus chòmhlan. Mar sheinneadair bhuannaich i na Puirt ann an 2011, agus sheinn i ann am farpais crìochnachaidh a' Bhuinn Òir. B' e stiuiriche Còisir Lunnainn a bh' innte.

Sandy NicDhòmhnaill Jones
Profile of the Author

Sandy NicDhòmhnaill Jones was the winner of the Wigtown Poetry Prize (Gaelic Section) in 2013; she also received a special commendation at Wigtown in 2014 and 2012. In April 2014, She won Ireland's bilingual Col. Eoghain Uí Néill Poetry Competition/ Farpais Bhàrdachd na Cuairte, for poetry written in Irish Gaeilge or Scots Gaelic. The winning poem was published in Sabhal Mòr Ostaig's 'Sgrìobag na Seachdain', April 2014, and Uist's Am Pàipear, May 2014. She has had Gaelic poems published in 'Northwords Now' (Issue 24 Summer 2013) and 'An Guth', 2013.

Sandy NicDhòmhnaill Jones has just completed her first collection of Gaelic poetry for publication: 'Crotal Ruadh' ('Red Lichen'). This is an exciting new body of work on which she has worked in the last couple of years under the mentorship of Aonghas 'Dubh' MacNeacail, with support from the Scottish Book Trust/ Gaelic Books Council's New Writers Awards ('Duais Sgrìobhadairean Ùra'). She is very grateful to Aonghas for his support, as well as for encouragement from Rody Gorman, Meg Bateman, Màrtainn Mac an t-Saoir, Gillebrìde Mac 'IlleMhaoil, Máire Ní Annracháin, and other friends in literary and academic Gaeldom.

Sandy began writing poetry in Gaelic in 2007, having started learning Gaelic in 2000. She is actively involved in Gaelic music as a singer and clàrsach player. Sandy has regularly won literary prizes at the Royal National Mòd in recent years, including the New Song and Poetry competitions, as well as for musical arrangements for choirs and instrumental ensembles. She is also a Gold Medal finalist and winner of the Puirt-a-Beul competition, and a former conductor of the London Gaelic Choir.

Tha Sandaidh na cànanaiche gu proifeiseanta; tha i air Bòrd Sabhal Mòr Ostaig, agus bha i na ball agus àrd-oifigear Bòrd na Gàidhlig na bu thràithe. Tha ùidh air a bhith aice fad a beatha ann am bàrdachd, an dà chuid sgrìobhadh, agus eadar-theangachadh bho chànain eile, nam measg Gearmailtis agus Fraingis. Gheibh i tlachd mhòr às an dubhlan agus a' chleas le structuran traidiseanta agus cruth-ruitheam diofraichte, gu sònraichte airson òran. 'S e toileachas a th' ann dhi a-nis a bhith a' lorg 'guth a' Bhàird' aice fhèin.

'S e òraidiche poblach sgileil a th' innte, le eòlas farsaing a bhith a' dèiligeadh ris na meadhanan. Tha i air nochdadh air rèidio agus telebhisean.

Cheumnaich Sandaidh bho SMO ann an 2010 le Cert HE Gàidhlig, agus fhuair i HNC Music Performance bho OGE (Colaiste Beinn na Faoghla) ann an 2009. Cheumnaich i le MA bho Oilthighean Oxford, Harvard agus Lunnainn. Tha i air a bhith an sàs, na beatha proifeiseanta, ann an leasachadh eadar-nàiseanta tro bhuidhnean nan Dùthchannan Aonaichte, a' Cho-fhlaitheis agus buidhnean sòisealta, agus 's e comhairleach riaghlaidh agus roi-innleachd a th' innte. Tha i cuideachd fileanta sa Ghearmailtis agus Fraingis, le ùidh san Spàinnis agus cànain eile.

'S e Gàidheal a th' innte bho a sinnsirean air an dà thaobh, agus le dachaigh ann am Fròbost, Uibhist a Deas.

She is a professional linguist, a Board member of the Gaelic college in Skye, Sabhal Mòr Ostaig, and former board member and officer of the national Gaelic development agency, Bòrd na Gàidhlig. Sandy has a lifelong interest in poetry, having written many poems in English, and translated poetry from German, French and other languages. She is fascinated with the challenges of different metric and rhyme structures, especially the traditional forms for song. Sandy is now enjoying developing her stylistic identity within Gaelic bardic traditions.

She is an accomplished speaker and has extensive experience of dealing with media, including television and radio appearances.

Sandy graduated from Sabhal Mòr Ostaig in 2010 with a Cert HE with Distinction in Gàidhlig, and gained a HNC in Music Performance from UHI (Benbecula College) in 2009. She holds Masters degrees from Oxford, Harvard and London universities. In her professional life she has been engaged in international development through organisations of the United Nations, the Commonwealth and civil society; she is a governance and strategy adviser. She speaks fluent German and French, with good Spanish, and interest in other languages.

Sandy has Gael ancestry, and her South Uist home is in Frobost, a township with a strong Gaelic community.

Buidheachas

Fhuair mi taic agus brosnachadh air mo chuid bàrdachd agus sgrìobhaidh bho iomadh neach còir thar nam bliadhnaichean. Fhuair mi cuideachadh mòr bho grunn dhaoine agus bhuidhnean eile, gus an leabhar seo a thoirt gu buil. Bu mhiann leam mo thaing chridheil a thoirt dhuibh uile, oir tha mi gu mòr nur comain. Ma dhìochuimhnich mi neach sam bith, tha mi ag iarraidh an leisgeul agus a' toirt taing dhaibhsan cuideachd.

Bu thoigh leam mo bhuidheachas sònraichte a nochdadh dhan fheadhainn a leanas airson taic is spionnadh mòr a thug iad dhòmhsa:

- Aonghas 'Dubh' MacNeacail a thug dhomh comhairle phrìseil agus stiùir iùlmhor mar oide fon sgeama 'sgrìobhadairean ùra', agus a sgrìobh ro-ràdh ro-choibhneil airson an leabhair seo.
- Comhairle nan Leabhraichean agus Scottish Book Trust airson maoineachadh a chur ri sgeama sgrìobhadairean ùra.
- Rosemary Ward, John Storey agus Màiri NicCumhais aig Comhairle nan Leabhraichean, a thug misneachadh prìseil agus foighidinneach dhomh le gach ceum air mo shlighe.
- Agnes Rennie aig Acair agus Bòrd Acair a ghabh ris a' chruinneachadh seo agus a thug cothrom mo chiad leabhar fhaicinn ann an clò; agus mo mhìle thaing do sgioba Acair airson an taic agus an sgilean deasachaidh.
- Meg Bateman airson leughadh mionaideach a rinn i air dreach a' chruinneachaidh, agus molaidhean smiorail is toinisgeul a thabhann, a thug feabhas air.
- Gillebrìde Mac 'IlleMhaoil airson tòrr stiùir, taic agus fealla-dhà air an rathad-ionnsachaidh agam, agus airson ceartachadh pongail cùramach a rinn e air dreach a' chruinneachaidh seo.

Acknowledgements

I have received support and encouragement on my poetry-writing efforts from many kind individuals over the years. I have also had great assistance from several people and organisations in bringing this book to completion. I should very much like to thank you all sincerely, for I am greatly indebted to you. If I have omitted anyone, I offer them my apologies and thanks also.

I should like to offer my particular gratitude to those listed below for the considerable support and fortitude they provided:

- Aonghas 'Dubh' MacNeacail, who provided invaluable advice and wise guidance as my mentor on the 'New Writers' Prize' scheme, and who has written a most generous foreword to this book.
- The Gaelic Books Council and Scottish Book Trust for funding and supporting the New Writers' Prize.
- Rosemary Ward, John Storey and Màiri MacCuish at the Gaelic Books Council who provided patient and precious encouragement for me on every step of the journey
- Agnes Rennie at Acair Ltd and the Acair Board for accepting this collection for publication and thus granting me the opportunity of seeing my first book in print: and my huge thanks to the Acair team for their support and fine editorial skills.
- Meg Bateman for contributing a very detailed reading of a final draft of this collection, and for providing courageous and judicious suggestions for its improvement.
- Gillebrìde Mac 'Illemhaoil for much guidance, encouragement and good fun on my journey learning Gaelic; and for the detailed and careful proof-reading that he kindly provided on the draft of this collection.

- Rody Gorman agus Màrtainn Mac an t-Saoir, airson an cuid misneachd is molaidhean air mo rathad-sgrìobhaidh.
- Na britheamhan agus buidhnean-taic aig Fèis Leabhraichean agus Duais Bàrdachd Bhaile na h-Ùige, agus Duais Bàrdachd Col. Eoghain Uí Néill; agus na britheamhan aig Mòdan Nàiseanta agus Ionadail, a thug spèis do na h-oidhirpean litreachais agus ciùil agam.
- An luchd-teagaisg uile a thog gu ìre nas àirde, fhileanta agus ghnàthasaiche na sgilean Ghàidhlig agam, aig cùrsaichean agus clasaichean aig Sabhal Mòr Ostaig, City Literary Institute, Colaiste Telford, Colaiste Stow agus Fèisean.
- Càirdean agus co-obraichean ann an saoghal cànan agus ceòl na Gàidhlig, a' gabhail a-steach Bòrd na Gàidhlig, Sabhal Mòr Ostaig, An Comunn Gàidhealach, Comunn Gàidhlig Lunnainn, agus Còisir Lunnainn, gu h-àraidh Ailean Rothach, Iseabail Nic an t-Sagairt agus Mìcheal Hill.
- Na nàbaidhean agus càirdean coibhneil agam ann am baile Fhròboist agus Uibhist a Deas.
- Mo mhàthair nach maireann: bha fìor thàlant agaibh air bàrdachd, agus guth binn.
- M' athair nach maireann: ruith ceòlmhorachd nur cuislean.
- Katy mo phiuthair chòir agus John mo chèile ghaolaich, a thug an taic agus creideamh buan dha na h-oidhirpean sgrìobhaidh agam.

- Rody Gorman and Martin MacIntyre for raising my spirits and providing advice on my journey as a writer.
- The judges and supporting organisations of the Wigtown Book Festival and Poetry Prize, and the Col. Eoghain Uí Néill Poetry Competition; and the judges at national and regional Mòds for valuing and encouraging my literary and musical endeavours.
- All those who have taught me Gaelic and raised my levels of fluency, idiom and expression, in studies and courses at Sabhal Mòr Ostaig, the City Literary Institute, Telford College, Stow College and Fèisean.
- Friends and collaborators in the Gaelic language and music world, including Bòrd na Gaidhlig, Sabhal Mòr Ostaig, An Comunn Gàidhealach, Comunn Gàidhlig Lunnainn, and London Gaelic Choir, especially Alan Munro, Iseabail Mactaggart and Michael Hill.
- My wonderful neighbours and friends in Frobost and South Uist.
- My late mother: you had a special bardic gift, and a lovely singing voice.
- My late father: musicality flowed in your veins.
- My dear sister Katy, and my beloved partner John, who have provided unfailing support for my writing, and have always believed in me.

Clàr-Innse

Table of Contents

Ro-ràdh le Aonghas 'Dubh' MacNeacail

Nuair a chuir mise eòlas air sgrìobhaidhean cruthachail Sandy NicDhòmhnaill Jones an toiseach, bha e air a bhith soilleir dhomh (mura b' e gun robh fios agam mar thà) gun robh i na seinneadair. Oir bha na h-òrain a sheall i dhomh, ann am pòsadh fonn is facal, cho coileanta 's a dh'iarras: bha siùbhlachd deiseil anns an ruitheam, agus seirm impidheach ann am fonn nam facal.

Mura robh na dàin, aig a' chiad shealladh, buileach cho deiseil; bha e fhathast follaiseach gun robh blas, agus brìgh na bàrdachd a' ruith tro gach oidhirp a chunnaic mi.

Chaidh bàrdachd is beachdan air ais is air adhart fad na bliadhna a bha mi air m' fhastadh mar chomhairliche dhi, agus is dòcha gun do thog mi ceist bho àm gu àm, mura robh mi cinnteach air a h-amas ann an dàn àraid, no gun tug mi stiùir bheag dhi, far an robh mi faicinn dòigh anns an gabhadh soilleireachadh a dhèanamh.

Tha i comasach, nuair a tha e iomchaidh, air tionndaidhean annasach, uaireanan èibhinn no clisgeach a thoirt air smuaint na bàrdachd. Mar eisimpleir, ann an sreath de dhàin stèidhichte air cuairt a ghabh i gu Eilean Mhauritius tha i a' cruthachadh cànan ùr – Gàidhlicréol: tha Gàidhlig agus Fraingis àraid an eilein (ris an abrar Créole) air am fighe còmhla ann an nòs macaronach, a' toirt tionndadh a bharrachd dhan Chréol fhèin (agus a' toirt tarraing air Ùisdean MacDhiarmaid anns an dol-seachad).

Ged a bhios i dèanamh mòran siubhail, tha na h-Eileanan Siar daonnan ga tarraing, agus gu h-àraid Uibhist. Agus 's ann le sùil a tha measail gun a bhith buileach drùidhte ann an riatanasan na sgìre is urrainn dhi mothachadh do chrodh Àisgeirnis ag

Foreword by Aonghas 'Dubh' MacNeacail

When I first became acquainted with Sandy NicDhomhnaill Jones' creative writing, it was clear to me (as though I already knew) that she was a singer. For the songs she showed to me were as fully-formed as could be wished in marrying tune to words: the rhythms flowed readily, and the word-cadences had a convincing ring to them.

As for her poems – from the very first reading, they were just as accomplished; it was already clear that the idiom and meaning of poetry coursed through every piece of her writing that I read.

Poems and ideas simply flowed back and forth between us, throughout the year when I was commissioned to act as her mentor, and perhaps I periodically raised the odd question, if I wasn't certain what she intended in a particular poem; or I made a suggestion, where I could see a way to make something clearer.

She has a well-judged touch for adding unusual, and sometimes witty or skittish twists to the concepts in the poetry. For example, in a series of poems originating in a visit she made to the island of Mauritius, she invents a new language – 'Gaelicréole': weaving together Gaelic and Créole – the variant of French spoken there – in a macaronic manner, adding a further twist to the Créole itself (and even making a passing reference to Hugh Macdiarmid en route).

Despite travelling widely, she is continually drawn back to the Western Isles, and particularly to Uist. With a respectful gaze – and without becoming too bogged down in the exigencies of local life – she fancifully imagines the Askernish cattle learning to play golf on the machair golf-course, where use of the common

ionnsachadh goilf a chluich air a' mhachair far a bheil casg air a chur air an ionaltradh. Tha tomhas snog ann an aoireadh na còmhstri fhillte eadar chluicheadairean caran leibideach agus crodh ro-eòlach air an àrainn: tha an t-amas air a targaid pongail agus eirmseach, ach gun fhanaid chruaidh, gun mhaoithneas.

Nuair a tha an àireamh 666 ag èirigh ann an crannchur-gill aig cèilidh (airson botal de dh'fhìon saor suarach...) cluinnear tarraing anail glacte measg na tha làthair, leis gu robh an dearbh àireamh air a chunntas ann an ois-chreideamh, ris an Deamhan fhèin. Gun a bhith bualadh tuilleadh is trom air a' chùis, tha am bàrd a' gabhail cothrom suathadh air smuaintean nas leatha, toirt a-steach Faust agus Gretchen – esan a tha dèanamh bargan leis an Droch Fhear, agus ise, nach robh ro neoichiontach nas motha – ach tha am botal ud a' tabhann faochaidh dhuinn.

Gheibhear òran do Thìr a' Mhurain, ach tha i cheart cho comasach air siubhal gu taobh eile an t-saoghail, leis a' phasgan a tha i tarraing de Haiku Callainn Shaigon – feargach, ceòlmhor agus, mu dheireadh, rèiteachail. Is, mar is minig a thachras, gheibh sinn dlùth-dhàimh eadar ghnàthalachdan gach ceàrn dhen t-saoghal, fada bho chèile 's gum biodh iad.

Chithear mar a tha i ag eadar-theangachadh tiotal an dàin, 'Cas/Cruaidh' leis na faclan ceangailte, 'AngrySteepFeet/CruelHarbour', a' dèanamh follaiseach (anns an dòigh a tha Rody Gorman air a bhith cleachdadh ann an cumantas, bho chionn ùine) gu bheil i airson gun urrainn dhuinn gach ciall a tha paisgte anns gach facal a leughadh. Nuair a thèid gaol air seachran, bhiomaid an dùil gum biodh sgolb is dealg an fhaireachaidh a' brodachadh na seice gus am faigh ceathach na dìochuimhn' làmh an uachdair. Anns an òran a leanas, An Togarrachd Fhaoin, tha an cuspair ceudna a' faighinn tionndadh eile, le faothachadh a' chiùil na leasachadh dhan tàmailt.

grazing has been restricted. There is a nicely-judged balance in the way she satirises the amateurish tourist go fers, contrasted with the cattle so deeply acquainted with the terrain: she strikes her target deftly and whimsically, without undue mockery or sentimentality.

When the number 666 comes up in a ceilidh raffle (for the prize of a rather cheap and inferior bottle of wine...), a sharp intake of collective breath is heard from the assembled company, because that very number was connected in popular superstition with the Devil himself. Without overly belabouring the point, the poet takes the opportunity to allude to associated ideas, including Faust and Gretchen – the bargain he strikes with the devil, and the doubt cast on her blamelessness – but that bottle offers some well-timed light relief.

There is a song written for Uist 'Land of the Marram-Grass'; but she is just as apt to fly off to the other side of the world, with a suite of 'Saigon Hogmanay Haiku' – fierce, musical and, ultimately, reconciled. And, as frequently happens, we're offered powerful affinities between orthodoxies in various corners of the world, however far apart they may seem.

It is clear from her translation of the title of the poem 'Cas/ Cruaidh' (the corresponding English words AngreySteepFeet/ CruelHarbour, demonstrating (in a way Rody Gorman has been deploying for some time) that she wants us to glean all the meanings wrapped in each word. When love goes off course, as in this case, we would naturally expect a thorny, splintered ambience that stings the poet, but finally disperses as the mists of forgetfulness prevail. In the subsequent song 'Futile Wishfulness', a similar subject takes a different turn, with the consoling effect of the music evolving into a warranted reproach.

Cha bhiodh e ceàrr a ràdha gu bheil i toirt bheusan a tha giùlan seagh daonna do bheatha an luis Crotal – cumhachd air a nochdadh ann an sia sreathan goirid, ach tha dùbhlan ann cuideachd, is i a' tomhas "sàr-chleas rag-mhuinealach/ na leantalachd". Agus saoilidh mi gum faod sinn an dàn seo a ghabhail mar shamhla air nàdar a' bhàird seo, i fhèin. Oir cha b' ann mar sgoilear òg a ghabh i da-rìreabh gu bàrdachd, ach aon uair 's gun do rinn i amas cha robh sìon a' dol a chur bacadh air a dìcheall airson a bhith strì gus a deòin a choileanadh.

Mar sheinneadair, tha i air a bhith eòlach air siubhal is seirm nan òran bho a h-òige: b' e rud eadar-dhealaichte bh' ann an tionndadh gu bàrdachd anns an "nòs ùr" (nach eil, is dòcha, cho ùr, ach nach eil càil nas fhasa). Agus tha an t-òranaiche seo cheart cho cofhurtail leis an fhacal a tha ri leughadh agus aithris is a tha i le rann an òrain.

Aonghas MacNeacail, 2014

It would be fair to say that she attributes human characteristics to the life-patterns of the plant 'Lichen': a strength that comes across in just six short lines, but also poses challenges, juxtaposing 'the ultimate obstinate tenacious feat/ of continuity'. And it seems to me that we could adopt this poem as a metaphor for the poet's own nature – for who she is. For it was not just that she discovered a real and studious urge to write poetry from an early age; but, once she had found her purpose, nothing would inhibit her quest to follow her muse.

As a singer, she developed an intuitive sense, from an early age, of the flow and cadence of structured song-form. It was something quite different to turn to 'new-style' free-form verse (which is perhaps not so new – nor any easier). And this maker of songs has now proved that she is just as comfortable with the written and spoken poetic word as she is with sung poetry.

Aonghas MacNeacail, 2014

I Sa chnoc-sìth

1 Na Fir-Chlis

A bhuannaich co-fharpais bàrdachd Corn. Eoghain Uí Néill 2014

Bha mise sa Chnoc-Shìth' o chunnaic mi thu 'n-dè
'S tha aithris neo-àbhaist' ri cur ann an sgeul
Mu na h-ainglean mallaichte, mur b' e gràs Dhè;
Na Fir-Chlis, na loisgich, a theab tuiteam on speur.

Chaidh teine 's an àil' a' lasadh gu geur
Le dealanach, sradagan, losgadh is leus.
Dhòirt na Fir-Chlis fuil theth às gach fèith,
'S nochd am manadh air olc: crotal-ruadh air na slèibh.

Chìthear mar mhallachd aig èirigh na grèin'
Fuil nan sàr-mhilidh, is fianais an creuchd:
Ach bheir blàr nan clis-threun ùr-fhadadh is dèin'
Do bhàrdachd nam filidh air sgrìobhadh fon seun.

Ach is mairg do dhream le dà-shealladh mar gheas
Oir cluinnear gu sìorraidh mac-talla is èigh
Nam Fir-Chlis, leth-uilc, a' milleadh 's an cleas
'S cha tig a chaoidh iochd orr', le cuireadh bhon eug.

I At the Knoll

1 'The Nimble Ones': The Northern Lights

Winner of Col. Eoghain Uí Néill Poetry Competition 2014

I have been at the fairy-knoll since we met yesterday
And of that I have a strange tale to relate
Of the angels who, had God not had mercy, were damned;
The Nimble Ones[1], fiery ones, who almost fell from the skies.

There was fire in the air, blazing fiercely,
Lightning bolts, sparks, flaming and flickering.
The Nimble Ones spilled hot blood from every vein,
And their presage of evil appeared; crimson lichen on the hillsides.

At sunrise you may witness this, like a curse,
The blood of the arch-warriors, proof of their wounds:
But the battle of the nimble fighters rekindles and intensifies
The bards' poetry, composed under their spell.

Yet woe betide those born with the sorcery of second-sight,
For they will for ever hear the echoes and cries
Of the Nimble Ones, the half-evil ones, playfully despoiling,
Who will never receive clemency, in the form of death's call.

---

1 In Fr. Allan Macdonald's 'Gaelic Words and Expressions from South Uist and Eriskay', the Northern Lights – the 'nimble ones' – are described as the angels who had been cast out from heaven and were falling thence, when God stayed his own hand. They were thus left forever suspended in the sky, fighting and spilling blood that appears the next day as **red lichen** on the stones, a presage of bad weather or worse evil to come. Their cries are sometimes heard echoing on earth by those attuned to such things.

2 Geaco Mascarene[2]

A bhuannaich co-fharpais bàrdachd Baile na h-Ùige 2013

sùilean geura
teanga leanailteach
foighidinn-acrais
cuimse nach diùlt.
meanbh-shealgair
air do chasan beaga clise
bun-os-cionn air mullach-rùim
a' leum as dèidh meanbh-chuileig
's gach mion-bhìdh 's air sgiathan:
neo a' feitheamh, ro-chiùin
's e neo-fhaicsinneachd do rùn
mar gum biodh tu reòthta.

craiceann trìd-shoilleir
bàn-dhearg chartreuse
chìtheadh do stamagan
troimhe – agus d' acras.
ith, ith air do shocair
laoigh, lìon fiù 's do chraos
dèan fleadh-frìde le furan:
bhiodh a h-uile biastag a dh'itheas tusa
gam bhìdeadh gu nimheil
'S gam ghlamhadh gu geòcach –
do chacag làn phlaosgan
a' dearbhabh nach dèan iad
tuilleadh cron ormsa.

---

2 Na h-Eileanan Mascarene – ainm grunn eileanan sa Chuan Innseanach, a' gabhail a-steach Mauritius, Seychelles agus Réunion.

2 Mascarene[3] Gecko

Winner of the Wigtown Gaelic Poetry Prize 2013

beady eyes
sticky tongue
patience of hunger
and reliable aim.
tiny hunter
on your nimble little feet
upside down on the ceiling
rushing at midges
and any small winged food:
or waiting, stillness itself,
invisibility your intent
as though you were frozen.

transparent skin
of rose and chartreuse
your little stomach visible
through it – and your hunger.
eat, eat at your leisure,
poppet, even gorge yourself,
take a welcome insect-feast:
every wee beastie you eat
would otherwise bite me viciously
and devour me voraciously –
your little droppings full of carapaces
proof that they
can no longer harm me.

---

3 The Mascarene Islands – name given to the group of Indian Ocean islands including Mauritius, Seychelles and Réunion.

chreutair bhig shnoig
is tusa nam chaidreabhach
chreutair bhig ait
is caomh leam thu
is d' anabarr-acrais.

handsome little creature
you are my ally
chipper little creature
i am fond of you
and of your inordinate hunger.

3 Eas

Moladh sònraichte aig co-fharpais bàrdachd Baile na h-Ùige 2012

is tusa an t-eas
a steallas orm,
a shruthas orm,
thusa an tuil
a shluaisreas,
a shlugas,
a shileas,
a bhogas
agus mise
rùisgte
air mo thumadh
air mo sguabadh leat.

is tusa an t-eas
a phronnas
a' chlach ìotach ro-dheònach
do bheum-slèibhe
neo-cheannsaichte caomh
gam chnàmh-chagnadh gu truasail
gam bhrùthadh gu tlùsail

do chumhachd gun choimeas
seasmhach suairc
uidh air n-uidh a' cur
gu socrach gu coileanta
ath-chumadh orm.

3 Waterfall

Special Commendation at Wigtown Gaelic Poetry Prize 2012

you are the waterfall
that splashes me,
flows over me,
you, the flood
that surges,
submerges,
pours over
and drenches me,
and me
stripped bare
held under
and swept away by you.

you are the waterfall
pounding down
on thirsty over-willing stone
your torrents
of unrelenting kindness
eroding me with compassion
pulverizing me with tenderness

the unmatched power
of your steadfast generosity
over time steadily
and completely
remaking my form

is tusa an treòir
a bhuadhachas fa dheòidh
le a foighidinn, a rùn, a reachd truacanta

agus mise
ath-shradach
soillseach
air mo ghlan-nighe
ùraichte slànaichte
cruth-atharraichte.

is tusa an t-eas
agus seo do thoradh:
an snaidheadh a dhearbhas
mo thaing sàr-mhaireannach.
o thusa, sil orm
gu sìorraidh bràth.

yours is the force
that ultimately prevails
with its patience, its purpose, its pitying passion

and me now
fresh sparkling
luminous
washed clean, purified,
whole again,
transfigured.

you are the waterfall
and this is your work:
the sculpted proof
of my everlasting gratitude.
pour thou onto me
for all time yet to come.

4 Crotal

Moladh sònraichte aig co-fharpais bàrdachd Bhaile na h-Ùige 2014

A' cumail
grèim air cloich
mar ghlacadh os-fhiadhaich
agus a' cluich
sàr-chleas rag-mhuinealach
na leantalachd.

4 Lichen

Special Commendation at Wigtown Gaelic Poetry Prize 2014

Keeping
a grip on stone
like a super-fierce embrace
and playing
the ultimate tenacious feat
of continuity.

II Fonn nam Facal: na Dàin

5 Òran Chòisir nan Gàidheal

Mar chomharrachadh air sia fichead bliadhna a' Chomuinn Ghàidhealaich agus Còisir Lunnainn

Sèist: Seinnibh na h-òrain bhinn!
Ceòlmhor is cridheil sinn;
Leantainneach thar nan linn
Th' ar cànan, ar ceòl, 's sinn fhìn.

Rann 1:
Togaidh sinn fonn ar sinnsre
San àm ri teachd le miann;
Chùm sinn ar sealbh le dìlse
Thar sia fichead bliadhn'. **Sèist**

Rann 2:
A' cumail ar sgeòil nar cuimhne,
Cuiridh sinn cliù an cèill
Ar còisire beò is pròiseil:
Seo cuirm ar bliadhna-fhèill. **Sèist**

Rann 3:
Ar beartas a tha ro-phrìseil –
Seann òrain nan Gàidheal;
Fàgaidh sinn ceòl ar dìleib
Don ghineil thig às ar dèidh. **Sèist**

Rann 4:
Togaibh an dàn gu sunndach
Le gàirdeachas gu h-àrd.
Cinnidh na Gàidheil san dùthaich
Is cluinnidh sibh guth ar bàird. **Sèist**

5 The Song of the Gaelic Choirs

Commemorating 120 Years of An Comunn Gàidhealach and Còisir Lunnainn

Refrain: Sing the sweet songs!
We are rich in music and of good heart;
Abiding through the generations,
Our language, our music, our essence endure.

Verse 1:
We will sound the tunes of our forebears
Resolutely into the future;
We have been true to our inheritance
Through six score years. Refrain

Verse 2:
Keeping our story alive in our memory,
We will acclaim the repute
Of our vibrant and proud choir
In this our festive year of celebration. Refrain

Verse 3:
Our treasure beyond price –
The old songs of the Gaels;
We will leave our musical legacy
To the generations that follow. Refrain

Verse 4:
Raise this song of celebration
With rejoicing hearts.
The Gaels will thrive yet in this land
And the voice of our bards will ring out. Refrain

6 An Togarrachd Fhaoin

Rann 1
Chaidil mi raoir fo aislingean breislich
Ann an doille na h-oidhch', 's fuaim fhuar-ghaoith' a shèid,
Is thachair mi raoir riut nam bhruadar is ghèill mi
Ri do ghuth is do ghealladh – do chluaineas is bhreug.

Rann 2
An crònan a sheinn thu – gam tharraing fod gheasaibh
Le mìlseachd gun fhìrinn a chuir orm seun:
An dòchas a spreig thu nam bhroilleach – mar chleasachd –
'S mo dhìlseachd a shuaraich thu agus a thrèig.

Rann 3
Chaochail na h-aislingean 's shoillsich na speuran
A' sgiùrsadh nam dhùsgadh an togarrachd fhaoin,
Is dh'fhoillsich a' chamhanaich thruacanta a sèamadh:
Gun mi tuiteam chaoidh tuilleadh fo bhuaidh do ghaoil:
Is cha tuit mi chaoidh tuilleadh fo bhuaidh do ghaoil.

6 Futile Wishfulness

Verse 1

I slept last night in a confusion of dreams
In the darkness of night, with the sound of a cold wind blowing
And I encountered you in my dream, and succumbed
To your voice and your promise – your deceit and falsehood.

Verse 2

You lulled me with singing, luring me and bewitching me
With counterfeit sweetness that cast a spell on me:
The hope that you inspired in my breast – as a mere recreation –
And my constancy, which you debased and forsook.

Verse 3

The dreams faded away and the skies enlightened
Banishing, as I awoke, this futile wishfulness,
And the compassionate dawn unveiled her warning:
Never again to fall prey to your love:
And I shall never again fall prey to your love.

7 Gealach an Abachaidh

Thig na ràithean mun cuairt, mar ghluasad na cuibhle,
Cinnidh a' ghealach 's cha diùlt i dhol crìon;
Tràghaidh na tuinn is lìonaidh an t-sumainn,
Ach ciamar a dh'èireas nam anam-s' a' ghrian?

Bha gealach an abachaidh òr air an oidhch' ud,
Bàn-bhuidhe, lainnireach, leantainn a tràth;
Thog i do spiorad le a soilleireachd mhaiseach.
Ach b' e gealach an abachaidh manadh do bhàis.

O mo mhàthair, tha mise gun fhaochadh às d' aonais,
'S mi fhathast cho fàsail, cho falamh, 's cho faoin;
Ach cha b' è do mhianns' gum bithinn ro fhada
Gun aotromachd 's aighear, gun sheòl is gun stiùir.

Ged cho beòthail 's a bha thu, bha d' imeachd a' dlùthadh;
Ach tha sgeul againn fhathast ri fhighe 's ri inns'.
Till thugam, mo mhàthair, nuair thilleas a' ghealach ud,
'S chan fhaigh a chaoidh pailteas ar còmhraidh a' chrìoch.

7 Harvest Moon

The seasons come around like the turning of the wheel,
The moon waxes and wanes without fail.
The waves ebb and the tides rise again,
But how can the sun rise in my soul?

The harvest moon was golden that night,
Fair yellow, sparkling, obeying its appointed time;
It lifted your spirits with its beautiful brightness.
But that harvest moon was a portent of your death.

O my mother, I am without solace in your absence,
And still so desolate, so empty, so lost;
Yet you would not have wished me too long devoid
Of lightheartedness, happiness, energy purpose.

Animation was your very essence, though your passing was near;
And yet we still have so many stories to interweave and to tell.
Come to me again, mother, at the harvest moon's return,
And the richness of our discourse will know no end.

8 Tìr a' Mhurain

Do Shìm MacCoinnich nach maireann, a thug oideachas dhomh leis an òran seo.

Rann 1:
Ionad tèarmainn mo shinnsre, tìr mo mhiann,
Tìr smeòraich chlann Dòmhnaill, is tìr nan eun binn
'S i ìoc mo chianalais, 's i tìr na sìth',
'S tu faochadh m' aigne, Uibhist mo chridh'. **Sèist**

Tìr a' mhurain, sòlas m' anaim,
O thìr a' mhurain, sìth mo chridh'.

Rann 2:
Tillibh don tìr seo, a chuideachd mo ghaoil,
Far am bheil fàilte, fois sìorraidh is tàmh,
Is bithibh maill' rium san dachaigh shean-ùr,
'S sìnibh gu sèimh ann an suain a' bhàis. **Sèist**

Rann 3:
Cha b' e cheannach a rinn sibh, a mhàthair chòir,
Air ur coibhneas, ur misneachd, is neart ur dèoin,
Neo sibhse, athair, le buadhan an òir:
Ur foighidinn, suairceas is eirmse ur beòil. **Sèist**

Rann 4:
Eunlaith eutrom nan speur, dìleab mo bheath'
Sàr-sheirm dom spiorad, dom dhàn is dom rùn
Beò-chuimhne m' athar is mo mhàthar threun
A' neartachadh dàimh is ar freumhan gu dlùth;
'S iad maill' rium a-nis an tìr mo rùin. **Sèist**

8 Land of the marram-grass

Dedicated to the late Simon Mackenzie, who mentored my composing this song.

Verse 1:
Place of sanctuary of my forebears, land of my desiring,
Land of Macdonald's song-thrush, land of sweet-singing birds,
The cure of my longing, the land of peace,
You are balm to my spirit, Uist in my heart. **Refrain**

Land of the sea-marram[4], solace of my soul,
O land of the sea-marram, peace in my heart.

Verse 2:
Return to this place, my beloved kinfolk,
Where there is welcome, eternal rest and ease,
Settle here with me in our new-ancient home
And rest peacefully in the slumber of death. **Refrain**

Verse 3:
These traits were innate in you, dear mother,
Your generosity, encouragement, and strength of will,
And you, father, had virtues of gold:
Patience, gentleness, and your whimsical wit. **Refrain**

Verse 4:
Birds light-on-the-wing in the sky, a bequest to me in life,
True music to my spirit, destiny and purpose:
A living commemoration of my brave father and mother,
Closely affirming our affinity and origins –
And they will abide with me now in this land that I love. **Refrain**

---

4 Land of the sea-marram grass, poetic name for Uist.

9 Uibhist Fhuranach

Soraidh slàn dhut, a bhaile-mhòir chruaidh gun truas,
Thrèig mi do chiomachas dochannach dorch
On a dh'fhàg mi an àrainn a chuir orm cùram,
A' sireadh ionad sìochail, sònraichte, sorch.

'S tu ùrlar mo dhuain, 's tu fadal mo dhàin
Ann an Uibhist fhuranach tha m' aigne slàn.

A bhaile, dh'iarr mi mo shòlas is dhiùlt mi do dhòlas
'S do dhùbhlainneachd, leann-dubh, doirbheas is deòir,
Le 'm shùil air mo shonas, is mo chùl ri do dhonas;
Ann an Uibhist àlainn, tha mo spiorad saor.

'S tu ùrlar mo dhuain, 's tu fadal mo dhàin
Ann an Uibhist fhuranach tha m' aigne slàn.

Le èiginn agus brùthadh bha 'm baile air mo chlaoidheadh,
Nam aonar measg na gràisg ud, bha mo spiorad dùint'.
O eilein uaine, freastal dhomh do chomraich agus coibhneas;
Le 'd shòghalachd mar ìocshlàint, socraichidh tu mo shunnd.

'S tu ùrlar mo dhuain, 's tu fadal mo dhàin
Ann an Uibhist fhuranach tha m' aigne slàn.

9 The Welcome of Uist

Farewell to you, cruel and heartless metropolis,
I have escaped your dark injurious captivity
Leaving surroundings that distressed me,
And seeking a special, peaceful, bright place.

You are the refrain in my song and the longing in my verse-destiny[5]
In welcoming Uist, my mind is whole.

City, I sought my solace and rejected your melancholy,
Your defiance, dejection, adversity and tears,
Setting contentment highest, and repudiating your devilment;
In lovely Uist my spirit is free.

You are the refrain in my song and the longing in my verse-destiny
In welcoming Uist, my mind is whole.

With stress and brutishness the city was exhausting,
Alone among the madding crowd my spirit was shutting down.
O green isle, bless me with your sanctuary and kindliness;
With your curative abundance, you will be my calm and cheer.

You are the refrain in my song and the longing in my verse-destiny
In welcoming Uist, my mind is whole.

---

5 There are two words 'dàn': it can mean both 'poem'/'verse' and also 'destiny'. The ambiguity is deliberate.

Tha do mhachraichean 's beanntan, 's do chluaintean bòidheach
Na aighear agus sòlas dhomh, Uibhist àit' mo chrìdh;
Far an d' fhuair mi fallaineachd, fàilteachadh is faochadh
Air faiche foiseil Fhròboist, far am faigh mi sìth.

'S tu ùrlar mo dhuain, 's tu fadal mo dhàin
Ann an Uibhist fhuranach tha m' aigne slàn.

Your machairs and hills and your beautiful pastures,
Are joy and solace to me, Uist, your place in my heart;
Bestowing health, welcome and respite upon me
In the restful meadows of Frobost, where I find peace.

You are the refrain in my song and the longing in my verse-destiny
In welcoming Uist, my mind is whole.

10 Dàn Buan-Bhuidheachais

Rann 1:

Tha do ghealladh gam stiùireadh le fàinne ar fiughair:
'S tu m' fhasgadh 's mo thruacantas, m' fhadal 's mo thlùs,
'S tu an dòchas nam chridhe, 's tu saoidh dom spiorad;
'S le do phòg is do chniadachadh, fuirich dhomh dlùth.

Sèist:

Cheist mo chridh', 's tu m' ulaidh 's tu m' àgh
M' eudail phrìseil don tug mi mo ghràdh
Mo chèile rùnaichte, cuiridh mi 'n dàn
Mo bhuan-bhuidheachas dhutsa gu bràth.

Rann 2:

On a theich sinn air èiginn air deuchainn thoinnte,
Mairidh ar buidheachas, sìthte le mòr-ghràs
Gar snaidhmeadh ri chèile le miann co-roinnte
Gu tairis 's gu buan, 's sinn fighte ler gràdh.

Sèist:

Cheist mo chridh', 's tu m' ulaidh 's tu m' àgh
M' eudail phrìseil don tug mi mo ghràdh
Mo chèile rùnaichte, cuiridh mi 'n dàn
Mo bhuan-bhuidheachas dhutsa gu bràth.

Rann 3:

Is tusa sìor-sheirceil, 's tu gu lèir mo mhiann
Is tusa làn suairceis, 's tu coibhneil is caomh;
Is tusa an tèarmainn a bheir dhomh dìon
Agus tusa mo shàr-dhraoidh, 's tu iomlan mo ghaoil.

10 The Song of Eternal Gratitude

Verse 1:

Your promise guides me, and the ring marking our intentions:
You are my shelter and compassion, my longing and tenderness,
You are the hope in my heart, and the wise sage for my spirit;
And with your kisses and caresses, remain close by me.

Refrain:

Love of my heart, my beloved and my joy
My precious darling to whom I have given my love
Soulmate meant for me, I will compose for you
The song of my eternal gratitude.

Verse 2:

Since we but narrowly survived a grave ordeal
Our thanks endure – relief that, by grace, we were spared
Binding us together with mutual intent
Caringly, lastingly, woven together in our love.

Refrain:

Love of my heart, my beloved and my joy
My precious darling to whom I have given my love
Soul-mate meant for me, I will compose for you
The song of my eternal gratitude.

Verse 3:

You are ever kindly, the fulfillment of my hopes
You are gentility, gentleness and grace;
You are the refuge that affords me protection
You are my fine magician and the entirety of my love.

Sèist:
Cheist mo chridh', 's tu m' ulaidh 's tu m' àgh
M' eudail phrìseil don tug mi mo ghràdh
Mo chèile rùnaichte, cuiridh mi 'n dàn
Mo bhuan-bhuidheachas dhutsa gu bràth.

Refrain:

Love of my heart, my beloved and my joy
My precious darling to whom I have given my love
Soulmate meant for me, I will compose for you
The song of my eternal gratitude.

11 Ortha Crann nan Teud

A Shoirbheis, tog
am fiùran-fhonn
is sèid, a ghaoith
tro mheur nan crann.

Osann nam faillean –
èist ri am fuinn –
anail nan duilleag
fo sgèith na h-oidhch'.

Blàth air meangan
na maidne air chrith,
a' tàladh phuingean
gu òrain nan linn.

A' chlàrsach as binne,
's e guth na craoibh;
nach cluicheamaid air
ar sgeulachd-gaoil?

Tro theudan gleusta
shèid osaig nan rann
is sèist nan geugan,
crònan nan crann.

'S e cruit na coille –
na ceòlraidh brìgh;
is ceòl na cruinne
ar seirm is sìth.

11 Incantation of the Harp-Strings-Tree

Fair Wind, carry
the saplings' tune,
and whistle, wind,
through the trees' branch-fingers.

The sighing of the twigs –
hear their melodies –
and the leaves' breathing
under night's sheltering wing.

Blossom on branches
in the morning, fluttering,
lulling and luring musical notes
into the songs of generations.

The most sweetly-tuned clàrsach
is the voice of the tree:
may we not play on it
our story of love?

Through well-tuned strings
the verse-breeze will blow
and the branches' chorus,
the murmuring of the trees.

The forest-harp it is –
the muses' very meaning;
and the music of the spheres
is our harmony and peace.

III Aicill

12 Oideas

Do Aonghas Dubh MacNeacail, a' comharrachadh Aois a' Gheallaidh san Ògmhìos 2012

Sibhse air àrd-ùrlar
a' leughadh ur bàrdachd
oidhche aig an t-Sabhal
agus suainealas do-chreidsinneach orm.

Sin far an do thòisich mi
o chionn còrr is deichead air
na h-òrain phrìseil shinnsireil a thogail
is iadsan gam thàladh gam tharraing
do chànan rùnaichte mo thùis.

Sibhse a-nis gam oideachadh
le mo chiad sgiathalachd chugallaich
mar dhealain-dè
air ùr-bhreith is air sgèith
a' dìreadh air oiteagan socair
a' sireadh solas a' chànain
air sgiathan dathail a' bhàird.

Ma tha sibhse a' creidsinn
gur ruigsinneach dhòmhsa na binnean ud:

bidh laoidh-feasgair a' bhana-bhàird shean-òig
ag èirigh mar eunlaith ùra
air itean neo-ghnàthaichte aighearrach
a' lorg an iùil fo ur stiùir.

III Anticipating rhyme

12 Mentor

To Aonghas Dubh MacNeacail, to mark his 70th birthday – 'the promised age' – in June 2012

You upon the stage
reading your poetry
one night at Sabhal Mòr
and me in a state of dreamy incredulity.

It is here that I started
more than a decade ago
to find the precious songs of my forebears
their songs alluring and luring me, as was to be,
to my ancestral language.

You mentoring me now
in my first unstable flights,
like a butterfly
just transformed and on her first wing
rising on gentle gusts
seeking the sunlight of our language
on the many-hued wings of the bard.

If it is your belief
that those peaks are within my reach:

then the vesper-hymns of the old-young bardess
will rise like new birds
on unaccustomed joyous wings,
under your tutelage, seeking their star.

13 Urram agus Iomagain

Mise a' tilgeil tàmailt orm fhìn
nach do chuir mi fiù 's criomag, luinneig thugaibh
on a choinnich sinn fo sgàilean mòr bàrdachd Shomhairle
's nis an dàrna mìos seachad...

Dh'fhairtlich an t-urram orm:
sibhse gam oideachadh
agus mise ro-thoilichte air,
ach a' cheòlraidh agam diùid sgèanach.
Mise fo sgàth; agus ise na tost.
Mar chiontach sgrìobh mi criomagan an ceilt
ach criomagan neo-airidh
's nach do dhùraig mi chur thugaibh
(agus sibhse le gliocas gun a bhith air mo ruagadh idir).

Dhùisg mo chogais a chlisge an-diugh,
gam mhaslachadh le mo dhroch thaing dhuibh.
Ciall tapaidh trom orm, iomagain is roileasg.

Seo mo phasgan luideagan-luinneagan
le athchuinge ri ur treòrachadh.

13 Honour and Anxiety

Here I am reproaching myself
that I have not sent you even a brief verse or ditty
since we met under Sorley's capacious umbrella
and a second month has now already passed ..

I felt honoured, yet also overcome:
exceedingly glad
to have you as my mentor
yet finding my Muse shy and hesitant.
Me apprehensive; and she tongue-tied.
Feeling beholden, I penned a few furtive
and unworthy fragments,
but did not yet dare send them to you
(and you wisely eschewed pursuing them.)

My conscience reawoke today with a start,
reproaching me for my ingratitude to you.
I felt a braver purpose, joy confused with anxiety.

So here is my parcel of fragments and ditties
with an entreaty for your guidance.

IV Annas is aithne

14 Calman Choilm

"Ler cead, a Mhaighstir, cha robh an t-eun ach a' leantainn òrdugh."

Leasan an là:
Tha còir aig gach naomh air co-dhiù aon èirig-mheachainn.
Tè ion-roghnaichte nas fheàrr na fear. Amen.

Bha an calman a rèir coltais ceannsaichte
carson a bhiodh amharas air
le geug-ola na ghob

(ach bha a' phiostal
falaichte fon sgiath)

... tha an naomh saor o shnòtadh – neo imcheist ...

cò aig nach biodh earbsa air calman
ach bha -> cuimse -> ionnsaichte aige.

là air choreigin
air spiris air do ghualainn
a' dùrdail suaimhneas nad chluais
'gu fìrinneach fìrinneach tha mi 'g ràdh ribh...'

chuimsich e:-
loisg:-
bhuail:-
agus mharbh.

corp na h-èirig-mheachainn
sìnt' air an fhòd

IV The strange and the familiar

14 Columba's dove

"Beg permission, Master, the bird was just following orders, Sir."

Lesson of the Day:
Each saint is entitled to at least one scapegoat.
Preferably a female one, rather than male. Amen.

The dove seemed tame
why suspect a dove
or the olive branch in its beak?

(but the dove concealed a pistol
beneath its wing)

... the saint is exempt from any whiff of taint – or from compunction ...

who would not trust a dove? –
but the dove was a -> practised -> shot.

one day
it perched on your shoulder
cooing reassuringly in your ear
'truly I say thus unto Thee...'

it aimed:-
fired:-
struck:-
and killed.

the scapegoat's corpse
stretched on the sod

fo bhagairt ais-èirig
ach gun dùil
    aiseirigh

ach fhathast cha robh amharas aig neach eile
mun eòin
    air
        feall
            brath
p-ò-g Ioscarioit.

Seo soisgeul, a rèir eòin[6].

at risk of re-forfeiture
but not expecting
    resurrection

yet still no-one else suspected
the bird
    of
        treachery
            betrayal
Iscariot's k-i-s-s.

This is gospel, according to a bird.

---

6 Two Gaelic words – one a noun, one a name – with the same genitive case: this can therefore be read both as 'this is gospel, according to a bird', and also 'gospel, according to John'.

15 Iseabail

Iseabail ro-throm
air àrd-ùrlar a' Mhòid
a' stiùireadh na còisr' aic',
is a pàist' ri teachd aithghearr
fo rabhadh gun teachd
co-dhiù an-diugh fhèin.

An crònan-crios:
'Sìth greiseag, a chuilein, is èist
ri do shìol, do cheòl, is do thùs:
is lìonmhor rannan òran na foighdinn;
is mithich dhuinn fàilte ort mar shèist.'

15 Iseabail

Iseabail heavily pregnant
on stage at the Mòd
conducting her choir,
and her soon-to-be-born infant
on warning not to arrive
this very day, at least.

The pregnant-belly croon:
'Be quiet a short while longer, little love, and listen
to your lineage, your music, and your origins:
there are many verses to the song of patience;
and its refrain will be our overdue welcome to you.'

16 Cas/Cruaidh

Bhiodh tu an còmhnaidh
cho cas[7] orm sna làithean ud
ged nach do bhuair mi riamh thu
thusa a' leantainn do dheòin fhèin
do chridhe-sa tioram
's gam chumail ann am mì-chinnt.

Thilgeadh tu tàmailt orm
gun rabhadh gun adhbhar
spreadhadh tu gu h-obann
gam mhaslachadh
's gad mhaslachadh fhèin
gun rian gun chùis.

Is bhithinn a' faireachdainn
do chunnart a' ruith na mo chuislean
air sliabh cas d' fheirge
lean mi ri stùc do smachd
thusa a' cumail làmh an uachdair
's air èiginn
theab mi tuiteam.

Ach oidhche dhorch àraidh
bhrist mi a-mach
a' teicheadh
air casan clise
fàillidh.

16 AngrySteepFoot/CruelAnchor

You were always
so angry with me in those days
not that I ever provoked you
you were just following the promptings
of your own arid heart
and keeping me uncertain.

You would insult me
without warning or cause
you would explode suddenly
affronting me
and disgracing yourself
without sense or grounds.

And I would feel
your danger coursing in my veins
on the steep slope of your anger
I clung to the precipice of your control
with you keeping the upper hand
and I only narrowly
avoided tumbling.

But one dark night
I finally broke away
escaping
on nimble feet:
furtive.

---

7 Cas' can mean 'angry', 'steep' and 'foot'; 'cruaidh' means both 'cruel' and 'anchor'; and the words and meanings interplay here

Bha fàsach do chridhe
cho cruaidh tartmhor
is truagh leam
an ath thràill
a ghlacas tu.

Mi a' sireadh cala rèidh
is le pathadh cho mòr orm
airson spèis, airson ceist
airson cèile
truacanta.

Is mis' a-nis air cruaidh
san acarsaid
thlùsail.

The desert of your heart
was so cruel and parched
I pity
the next victim
you capture.

Then I sought a calm haven
and with such thirst
for affection, for a beloved
for a partner
capable of pity.

And I am now at anchor
in the harbour
of compassion.

17 Frìth Bhrìghde air an Inntinneas

Lean ri comhairle nan daoine
as cùramaiche riut
as càirdeile dhut
's as dèidheile ort.

Tha thu ann an cunnart oillteil
tha thu faisg air a' chreig
agus tusa cho cugallach
led inntinn far na meidh:

tha fuasgladh furasta
is e mar fhiachaibh ort
dìon a thairgse do chàich
agus fòir ort fhèin.

Fios fìrinn gun fios brèige:
tog do chothrom, fire faire
thoir an aire, faire, faire

'S mithich mithich mithich
Tog ìoc tog ìoc tog ìoc
Bi glic bi glic bi glic:

17 Bridget's Augury for the Ail-Mind

Follow the counsel of the people
who care most for you
bear you greatest friendship
and are fondest of you.

You are in dreadful danger
you are close to the precipice
you are so unsteady
with your mind off-balance:

there is a simple solution
and it is incumbent on you
to offer protection to others
and seek aid for yourself.

Message of truth and without falsehood:
seize your opportunity, fire faire
beware, take care, care

'Tis high time high time high time
Seek remedy remedy remedy
Be wise be wise be wise:[8]

---

[8] Bi glic bi glic – 'be wise be wise' – is how Gaels put onomatopoeic words to the cry of the oyster-catcher, whose name in Gaelic is 'Gillebrìce' or 'servant of St Bridget'. In Uist the name is 'Brìd-eun' (pronounced 'Brìdean'), or 'Bridget's bird'.

Ged nach seo ach comhairle, èist:
Mura còrd i riut, moladh;
Mura cluinn thu e, rabhadh;
Mura toir thu feairt air, òrdugh;
Mura cùm thu ris, èiginn;
Mura gèill thu rithe, aimhreit,
Fiù 's làmh làidir an lagh.

Tog do leigheas
diùlt d' inntinneas
lorg do mhaitheas.

Although 'tis but advice, listen:
If you like it not, a recommendation;
If you hear it not, a warning;
If you heed it not, an order;
If you obey it not, compulsion;
If you yield not, a riot,
Even the full force of the law.

Take your medication
repudiate your ail-mind
seek your better self.

18 Haiku Callainn Shaigon

I An Tuil: Tailm-Tàire

1 Fuachd
Chan fhaic thu ach fuil
chan fhairich thu ach fearg
chan fhiù e ach eug.

2 Breitheanas
Thig, là na cruinne
’s leag peanas air a’ pheacach
le cràdh oillteil mall.

3 Buil
Dh’fhuadaich e thu
’s le puinnsean do ghràin’ na chuislean
gheibh e fhathast sgrios dheth.

4 Creach
Do smaointean searbha
ga shealg mar pheilearan
astar a bheatha.

5 Dìoghaltas
Creithleag gad bhìdeadh
gu nimheil sgreamhail: gheibh i
buille-bàis od làimh.

18 Saigon Hogmanay Haiku

I The Deluge: Catapult of Contempt

1 Ice-Cold
You see only blood
you can feel only fury
his worth is but death.

2 Judgement
Come, day of judgement
and punish the sinner with
slow painful torment.

3 Consequence
He forced your exile:
your hatred poisons his veins
and will yet wreck him.

4 Ruination
Your bitter broodings
hunting him down like bullets
the length of his life.

5 Vengeance
The gadfly that stings
you with loathsome venom earns
death's blow from your hand.

II Muir-Làn: Tìde-Mhara

6 Talamh fàs

Driùchd a' sileadh deòir
air geugan sgapte briste
is craobhan leagte.

7 Ath-Leasachadh

Is tusa mi fhìn
A' toirt aithne dhut, truas,
'S an toirt a bha dhìth.

II High-Tide: Tide-Turn

6 Wasteland

Dew-drops weeping tears
on broken scattered branches
and on fallen trees.

7 Reclamation

Yes, you are me: pay
respect to yourself, pity,
and the regard due.

III An Traoghadh: Taisteal Leithis-Leòin

8 Fàire

Crith-thalmhainn chaithte
ach faire-fàir' na fairge:
oillt tsunami orm.

9 Eadar-theine

Saighdean lainnireach
gan losgadh cianail faisg orm
nam throm-laighe fhathast.

10 Am falach

Thoir cuilidh chiùin dhomh
saobhaidh far nach fhaotainn cron
gus am fàsainn slàn.

11 Tìr-ìoc

Blàth cùbhraidh lotus
oiteag Cuan Sìon' a Deas
Buddha, Vietnam, sìth.

12 Tarasque[9]

Bheir dràgon cumhachd
Leòmhann dìon, tearc-eun sìth,
's turtar beatha shlàn.

---

[9] 'S e 'tarasque' ainm air uile-bhèist mhiotasach san Òb Halong ann am Vietnam a Tuath, beagan mar 'Nessie Vietnam'. 'S e na ceithir creutairean-fortain sa chreideamh Bhuddhist a nochdas sa Haiku mu dheireadh seo.

III The Ebb-Tide: Wound-Healing Voyage

8 Horizon

Earthquake expended,
but watch the sea's horizon;
tsunami-dread still.

9 Cross-fire

Flaming arrows shoot
too painfully close to me
in my nightmares still.

10 In hiding

Show me a quiet lair,
haunt where no harm befalls my
growing whole again.

11 Healing land

Fragrant lotus bloom
Breeze of the South China Sea
Buddha, Vietnam, peace.

12 Tarasque[10]

The dragon brings power,
lion defence, phoenix peace
and turtle long life.

---

10 'Tarasque' is the name of a mythical monster in Halong Bay in North Vietnam, a little like a Vietnamese 'Nessie'. The creatures appearing in this last Haiku are the four creatures that bestow good fortune according to the Buddhist faith.

V Faiche Fhròboist

19 Cailleach-oidhche Fhròboist

Chaidh mi a-mach air oidhche chiùin bhòidhich Uibhist
a' sireadh deò agus sealladh
air gealach an abachaidh àlainn.
Gairm gheur
creutair a' leum bhon t-similear
is a' dìreadh san adhar dhubh,
sgiathan spracail a' bualadh an dorchadais.
Cailleach-oidhche air feagal fhaighinn
far an do shir i tèarmainn.
eun mòrail gam theicheadh
air sgiathan farsaing,
sgiathan draoidheil airgid le boillsgeadh na gealaich orra
faileas flathail a' seòladh às fhianais thar achaidhean Fhròboist.
Agus mise ann an uireasbhaidh duilich
mise fo bhròn gun do dh'fhuadaich mi thu.
Gabh m' aithreachas, eun òirdheirc;
lem uile chridhe cha bhithinn
airson d' fhois a ghoid.

V Frobost meadows

19 Frobost Owl

I went outside on a calm beautiful Uist night
for fresh air and a view
of a lovely harvest moon.
A shrill cry
a creature starting up from the chimney
and rising in the black air
powerful pinions beating the darkness.
An owl taking fright
where she had sought refuge.
A majestic bird fleeing from me
on wide wings
magical silver wings with the moonshine upon them
a splendid shadow sailing out of sight over the Frobost fields.
And I impoverished by my own action,
mourning that I drove you away.
Please accept my remorse, noble bird:
with all my heart, I would not have meant
to rob you of your peace.

20 Crodh Goilf Àisgeirnis

Machair àlainn Àisgeirnis
a mhothaich Seann Tom Morris ann an 1891
le innleachd tuill is buill a' tighinn a-steach air,
is sùil gheur air cumadh-tìre: dìreach ion raon goilf.

Cruinn-leum air adhart thar linn:
le faram is moit thèid
seann raon goilf chadalach Àisgeirnis a leudachadh.

Ach ged a gheibh an crodh a rugadh ann
cead fuireach air raon goilf (ma tha iad modhail)
agus fiù 's cumail feur na machrach ithe

fhuair na croitearan rabhadh cruaidh gun an crodh
buaireas a chur air na goilfearan air thuras
is iadsan a' pàigheadh an deagh sgillinn
gus na tuill àlainn eachdraidheil a chluich.

Crodh bochd Uibhisteach, an cridhe nan slugan,
a' tionnsgain gu clis cleasan ùra snog glic
mar mhearaiche a' toirt tlachd don luchd-turais:

20 The Golfing Cattle of Askernish

The beautiful Askernish machair
that Old Tom Morris noticed in 1891
devising a scheme involving holes and balls,
with his sharp eye for the lie of the land – ideally suited for a golf course.

A big leap, one century forward:
With pomp and fanfare
the sleepy old golf course of Askernish is to be re-launched.

And, though the cattle that were born there
are permitted to stay on the course (if they behave)
and even to keep grazing the machair grass

the crofters have been formally cautioned
not to let their cattle inconvenience the golf-tourists
who've paid their pretty penny
to play the lovely historic holes.

Pity the poor Uist cattle, with their hearts in their mouths,
swiftly devising clever and entertaining new tricks
like jesters trying to entertain the tourists:

dh'ionnsaich an crodh caman is ball a làimhseachadh
gu h-ealanta aotrom; cluichidh iad fhèin
gu tric toll-aon-bhuille, lorgaidh iad fiù 's
buill chaillte sa 'rough', gan tional is tilleadh
gu beulach-beusach do na coigrich beartach liobasta.

Am biodh Seann Tom toilichte, mòr às an fheabhas seo
neo an tuiteadh uamhann air? An dùisgeadh e san uaigh?

Bidh crodh Àisgeirnis a' cnuasachadh air a' cheist,
is a' cnàmhadh na cìr, gu cian nan cian,
na filidhean fialaidh feur-itheach fionnairidh.

the cattle have learned to wield clubs and balls
expertly and deftly; they can even
play a regular hole-in-one, and retrieve
balls lost in the rough, collecting and returning them
with feigned courtesy to the wealthy, inept intruders.

Would Old Tom be happy, proud of this progress,
or would it fill him with horror? Would he turn in his grave?

The Askernish cattle will be ruminating on the question
and chewing the cud for ages to come,
those warm-hearted, herbivorous, watchful minstrels.

21 Crannchur-gill Cheòlais

Cèilidh mhòr aig ceann seachdain Cheòlais
Deagh shunnd agus deagh fhonn
Crannchur-gill agus na duaisean
Gu bhith deiseil.

Bean an taigh a' togail na tiogaid mu dheireadh:
'Gorm a-sia a-sia a-sia'.
Dà dhiog fèath nan eun.
Plosg.
Anail ga tarraing leis a' choithional
mar le aon neach –
an neach mu dheireadh san t-saoghal.
Cuideigin a' tùchadh.
Gàire anfhoiseil.
Braoisgeil.
Làmh ga sìneadh an àird le tiogaid ghorm innte,
Guth beag: 'dè gheibh mi?'

21 Ceòlas Raffle

A big cèilidh at the end of Ceòlas week
high spirits and a happy mood
Raffle, and the prizes
almost finished.

The 'mistress of ceremonies' holding up the last ticket:
'Blue six-six-six[11].'
Two seconds of total silence.
A gasp.
A collective intake of breath by the congregation
as if by one person –
the last person on earth.
Someone coughs.
An uneasy laugh.
A giggle.
A hand raised up holding a blue ticket,
A small voice: 'what have I won?'

---

11 In Gaelic traditional thinking, 666 is the number connoting the devil.

Seadh, dè gheibh sibh,
le a-sia a-sia a-sia
a Mhaighstir Faust?
Cleas caillte
Cridhe ciùrrta
Cogais shalach
Beatha suaraichte
Gretchen mharbh
Dòchas trèigte
Cumhachd air glacadh leis an donas:
Lèirsgrios.

Neo, leis an tiogaid shònraichte seo,
gheibh sibh botal saor
fìon neo-shònraichte.
Slàinte!

Yes indeed, what have you won,
with six-six-six,
Mister Faust?
A game lost
A wounded heart
A filthy conscience
A life defiled
Gretchen dead
Hope betrayed
Power seized by the dev l:
Total ruination.

Or, with that special ticket,
You can have a cheap bottle
of very average wine.
Your health!

22 Sgiath-dheargan

A' bocadh mun cuairt
gur nighe fhìn ann an glumagan
a' piocadh nam mucagan agus fàileagan
air ròsan is drisean
doimhneachd a' gheamhraidh.

Sibhse an t-acras
sibhse nur n-aoighean agam
toradh lusan an fhearainn agam
di-beathte dhuibh
mar bheathachadh.

Fuirichibh rium
eòin spaideil
le miann-maireann annaibh.

Boillsgeadh sliosan dhearga
sibhse a' dìreadh le creach nur spuirean,
stiall-sùilean
mar sgàil-sùilean an reubair
is aodach breac-stiallach ciomaich oirbh

A mhearlaich-mhucagan èibhinn
goidibh ur sàth.

22 Redwings

Hopping about
bathing in puddles
pecking the last hips and haws
off wildroses and briers
in depth of winter.

You are hunger
you are my guests
welcome to the wild fruits
of my land
for sustenance.

Stay with me
dapper birds
imbued with spirit of survival.

Flashes of red flank
as you soar with your booty,
sporting eye-stripes
like the robber-brigand's mask
and speckle-striped jailbird attire.

Witty little haw-thieves
steal your fill.

23 Dina Arobi – An t-Eilean Fàsail: l'Île Déserte – quelques images

Maurice[12] *libre 2012 à quarante-quatre années: saorsa na dùthcha ann an ceathrad ceithir sreath*

Gàidhlicréol

('Boireannach sòbarra a' coimhead air an fhàinne-cluaise'[13])

sirandane, tomhais? sampek – innis dhuinn!
itheamaid, tapeta: manzons – slàinte mhath!

zoli zoli kado – saor is an asgaidh
tiodhlac brèagha – à zoli zoli prix!

sega, en ba! c'est ça –
abair fealla-dhà ma-tà!

konmela, eskiz, le fait noir:
mo leisgeul a-nis – oidhche mhath!

Smuain shùgrach

thèid mis' is tusa do Phamplemousse[14]
jardin nan lusan tropiques nan dusan

12 An t-Eilean Fàsach, ainm a chuir malairtich Arabaich air Mauritius, nach deach aiteachadh aig an àm sin.

13 'Boucle d'oreille', (trochetia boutoniana) flùr nàiseanta Mhauritius. Cleas-iomradh air an dàn 'A drunk man looks at the thistle' le Ùisdean MacDhiarmaid.

14 Pàirc nàiseanta lus tropaigich Mhauritius, stèidhichte anns an 18mh linn mar phàirc prìbhideach le Mahé de Labourdonnais agus leasaichte sna 19mh linn mar 'arboretum' leis na Bhreatannaich; air ùr-ainmeachadh airson Sir Seewoosagur Ramgoolam, stèidheadair neo-èisimeileachd Mhauritius.

VI A Far Side

23 Dina Arobi – The Deserted Isle: l'Île Déserte – some images

Independent Mauritius[15] 2012 – at forty-four years, in forty-four lines[16]

Gaelicréole
('A sober woman looks at the ear-ring[17]')

sirandane, guess? sampek, go on, tell!
let's eat, tapeta: manzons, good health!

zoli zoli kado – and almost for free
such a pretty present – à zoli zoli prix!

sega, en ba! c'est ça –
what fun this is, tra-la!

konmela, eskiz, le fait noir:
beg pardon, I'm off now, bonsoir!

Lighthearted reflection

let's go, you and I, to Pamplemousse[18],
jardin of flowers tropiques and profuse

---

15 'Deserted Island', early name given by Arab traders to the (then uninhabited) island of Mauritius.
16 The choice not to translate the French/créole into English was deliberate, to preserve the macaronic essence (interwoven bilingual form) of this poem, including its rhymes and metres.
17 'Ear-ring', the national plant of Mauritius. Playful reference to the poem 'A drunk man looks at the thistle' by Hugh MacDiarmid (Christopher Murray Grieve).
18 National tropical botanical gardens of Mauritius, founded in the 18th century as a private park by Mahé de Labourdonnais and developed into an arboretum by the British in the19th century; renamed for Mauritian independence leader, Sir Seewoosagur Ramgoolam, after his death.

is fàgaidh sinn volontiers leithid Souesstrok[19]
do dh'amadain fhuadain le fada cus stoc
daoine gun toinisg gun toirt 's gun deagh ghnè
's nach toir fìor-mheas air Maurice belle et vraie.

fàgamaid iad sur les plages de sable
airgid, lainnireach, sans nier agréables –
nager dans les ondes sa mhuir ghorm-leug
leis na leumadairean-mara – (apprivoisés....)

Lotus ceithir-chànanach

tha ceithir taobhan aig a' chuimhneachan Ramgoolam[20]
a stèidhich an rìoghachd l'Île Maurice libre,
's ghràbhailt' air a bhunait tha ceithir cànain
beurla, frangais, hindi agus sìnis:

's air gach taobh an dearbh theachdaireachd buidheachais
de ses compatriotes, le làimh fialaidh sìnt' –
mar shamhla eugsamhlachd 's iomathùsachd:
is lotus air, suaicheantas sìorraidheachd 's sìth.

---

19 Ainm faoinsgeulach airson baile-turasachd daor (agus dùinte don na dùthchasaich).
20 Air a thogail anns a' phàirc Phamplemousse, le gàradh-meòrachaidh faisg air, air a bheil 'samadhi' (Sanskrit - 'samhchair-inntinn' yoga).

and leave volontiers the Souesstrok[21] kind of thing
to the vapid rich tourists with far too much bling
but no culture, no breeding, no sense how to pay
the respect that is due to Maurice belle et vraie.

let's leave them now sur les plages de sable
silvery, glittering, sans nier agréables –
nager dans les ondes in the sapphire sea-spray
with the wave-leaping dolphins – (apprivoisés.. .)

Quadrilingual lotus

the Ramgoolam monument[22] presents its four faces
marking the birth of l'Île Maurice libre,
and graved on its plinth are the tongues of four places
english and french, chinese and hindi:

and on each of the facets the same thankful tribute
de ses compatriotes, hands stretched in gratitude
for diversity and freedom, expressed in this symbol –
the lotus-flower's eternally peaceful attitude.

---

21 Fictitious name of expensive 'fortress' (closed-compound) tourist resorts.
22 Monument erected in Pamplemousse gardens next to garden of remembrance named 'samadhi' (Sanskrit for complete yogic stillness-of-mind).

Dùrachd

na dreamannan measgte de tout coin du monde
a thugadh a-nall, sans bien comprendre
quelle espoir d'avenir, ou quel cauchemar de sort
les attendît san eilean seo, fad' o thìr mhòr

mélange en outre de langues, teanga is gnàths
bha teanntachd is tràillealachd orra an tùs:
ach thàinig saorsa, fèin-mheas, croissance,
une communauté de plus en plus

devenue cohésive, mature, à l'aise
attirant visites, luchd-tadhail nan ceudan
don dùthaich bheannaichte thorrach gu deas
sa chuan innseanach, innsean nan seudan.

chan ann falamh an-diugh tha an talamh
chan e tìr fhàsail a-nis th' anns an innis
ach tarraingeach 's taitneach, eilean an draoidh

l'île magique magnifique Maurice
samadhi[23], satori, bénie de délices
c'est pardes[24], serendip – prestidigité.

---

23 Bun-bheachd Zen 'àite gun chrìoch', coltach ri 'samadhi' yoga.
24 Pardes - Eabhrach agus Arabach air 'gàradh'/"ubhal-ghort', agus tùs an fhacail 'Pàrras'.

Sincere goodwill

:he many tribes mingled de tout coin du monde
who had been brought here, sans bien comprendre
quelle espoir d'avenir, ou quel cauchemar de sort
es attendît ici, far from their native shore.

mélange en outre de langues, customs and tongues,
slavery their early lot, and cruel abuse:
out freedom arrived, self-respect, croissance,
une communauté de plus en plus

devenue cohésive, mature, à l'aise
attirant visites, and tourists in droves
to the isle in the south seas, fertile and blessed
like jewels on the waves and gems in the coves.

this isle is no longer 'the desolate place',
not barren, but full of abundance and grace
beguiling, enchanting, the star-dusted isle:

l'île magique magnifique Maurice
samadhi, satori[25], bénie de délices
c'est pardes[26], serendip[27] – prestidigité.

---

25 In Zen Buddhism, 'infinite space' similar concept to yogic 'samadhi'.
26 Hebrew and Arabic for 'garden'/'orchard', and or gin of the word 'paradise'.
27 Serendip, originally Arabic, 'happy accident'/'pleasant surprise' (also attrib. Tamil, orig Sanskrit, 'golden isle', old name for Sri Lanka).

24 Iadsan an teachd: l'avenir, c'est eux

12/3/2012 – 44mh là neo-èisimeileachd Mhauritius

deugairean donna dubha
de gach dream às an dùthaich
a' snàmh sna tuinn
tràigh phoblach a' Bhàigh Ghuirm
a' togail phioramaidean daonna
a' dìreadh air guaillnean a chèile
a' gàire 's ag èigheach
a' tarraing às a chèile
a' tuisleadh is tuiteam
a' togail às ùire.

là saor là sonraichte
là gàire là gàirdeachais
là meòrachaidh
là neo-èisimeileachd
nàisean Mhauritiius
beannachdan oirbh
muinntir innis-mire
nach muladach mise
ur fàgail a-màireach.

24 They are the future

12/3/2012 – 44th Anniversary of Mauritius' Independence

teenagers brown and black
from every ethnicity of this land
swimming in the waves
of the public beach at Blue Bay
building human pyramids
climbing on each other's shoulders
laughing and shouting
teasing each other
tumbling and falling
and building up afresh.

a day off, a special day
a day of laughter a day of celebration
a day for reflection
independence day
of the nation of Mauritius
health and blessings to you
people of the cheerful island
mine is the sadness
to be leaving you tomorrow.

25 Nighean bheag san t-saoghal bhochd

Meal do shaorsa, m' eudail bhig,
Oir cha bhi i fada agad.

Cha bhi fèileaganaich is faireachdainn
Ceadaichte dhut fada gu leòr,
Ach fuil is fulang is ionndrainn fhaoin.

Bidh na fir a' cur smachd is impidh ort
Is a' diùltadh do dhòchas,
Is thèid do phòsadh dhad aindeoin.

Meal do shaorsa, m' eudail:
Bidh feum agad air do chuimhneachan
San àm aimrid ri teachd.

25 A small girl in the poor world

Enjoy your freedom, little darling,
it will not long be yours.

Playful frolics and feelings
Will not be granted you long enough,
But instead, blood and suffering and unfulfilled longings.

Men will impose their will and force upon you
And deny you your hopes,
And you will be married off against your will.

Enjoy your freedom, darling:
You will need your memories of it
In the barren time to come.

VII Faire-fàire

26 Cridhe ùr

Fhuair e cridhe ùr an-diugh
cridhe fuadain
ach spionnadh ùr
o chuideigin
a chaill a bheatha-sa
ach a thug dha
an tiodhlac as prìseile
san t-saoghal.

Saoil:
eil a leithid-sa
nam cheann,
nam cholainn-sa
no nam chridhe?

VII Watching the horizon

26 A new heart

He received a new heart today
an alien heart
but new strength
from someone
who lost their own life
but gave him
the most precious gift
in the world.

I wonder:
is there anything equal to this
in my head,
in my own body
or in my heart?

27 An aghaidh na h-obair nodha

*(u***n – le taing do Shìlis)*[28]

ciamar a shaoileadh tu
cuspair a theagasg
gun chruth neo rian?
'S ann aig cridhe cànain
a tha gràmar:
cànan a theagasg gun ghràmar?...
am muineadh tu
bith-eòlas gun mhoileciuil,
nàdar-fheallsanachd gun chumhachd-tarraing,
eachdraidh gun chinn-latha neo tachartasan,
ceòl gun fhonn 's gun bhuille?

neo gaol gun chridhe
beatha gun anail
crìoch gun tùs
facal gun bhrìgh
brìgh gun chànan:
mar sin, cànan gun ghràmar?
obair nodha, mìnich do luach:
ciamar a ghleusas tusa na cruinnean?

---

28 Ùmhlachd don a' bhana-bhàrd Sìleas na Ceapaich.

27 Against the new work

*(u***n – with thanks to Cicely)*[29]

how would you think
to teach a subject
without structure or method?
at the very heart of language
is grammar:
to teach a language without grammar?...
would you teach
biology without molecules
physics without gravity,
history without dates or events
music without melody or rhythm?

or love without heart
life without breath
end without beginning
word without meaning
meaning without language
and thus, language without grammar?
new work, explain your worth
how will you tune the spheres?

---

29 A homage to the female bàrd Sìleas MacDonald.

28 Mallachd charminadelica air a' ghalar-clèibh

Le leisgeul do Alastair MacGilleMhìcheil[30]

1 Asparain duibh

Gur mis' th' air mo chràdh
Leis a' ghalar-clèibh
A thàinig gun chuireadh
Is le mì-rùn air m' eug.

Aspairin duibh *o hi o ho*
antibiotaica charminadelica
mise fo mhulad *ro hu ill o*
casadaich sgràthail *o ho bha hu*
thalla, mo mhallachd ort!
asparain duibh.

Gur mis' th' air mo chràdh
Leis a' ghalar-clèibh
A thàinig gun chuireadh
Is le mì-rùn air m' eug.

Aspairin duibh *o hi o ho*
antibiotaica charminadelica
mise fo mhulad *ro hu ill o*
casadaich sgràthail *o ho bha hu*
thalla, mo mhallachd ort!
asparain duibh.

30 Chruinnich MacGilleMhìcheil 'Ortha nan Gàidheal' – 'Carmina Gadelica' – agus 's e cleas-fhacail air an tiotail laideann a rinn mi.

28 A carminadelic imprecation upon the bronchitis

With apologies to Alexander Carmichael[31]

1 Black Aspirin

It is I that am pained
with the bronchitis
that came uninvited
maliciously intent on my death.

Black aspirin, *o hi o ho*
Carminadelica antibiotica
O how sad I am *ro hu ill o*
Cough's destructiveness *o ho bha hu*
Be away, my curse on you,
Black aspirin!

It is I that am pained
with the bronchitis
that came uninvited
maliciously intent on my death.

Black aspirin, *o hi o ho*
Carminadelica antibiotica
O how sad I am *ro hu ill o*
Cough's destructiveness *o ho bha hu*
Be away, my curse on you,
Black aspirin!

---

31 Carmichael collected the "Songs and Charms of the Gaels" and it's Latin title 'Carmina Gadelica' invited psychedelic word-play!

2 Tobhta mo shlàinte

Tobhta mo shlàinte air na blàraibh
tùchadh is smùcanaich fad' an là!
ho a ho thalla, tha mis' air mo chràdh
ho a ho thalla, o thalla gu math!

Trì nèapraigean 's srùbagan 's trì uisge-beath'
an sreothart a' srannartaich, thig mo sgrios dheth!
ho a ho thalla, o thalla gu lèir
an deamhain is olc ort, a ghalair-clèibh!

3 Rann Prìosan-Tinneis

O is garbh an sgleò, is mis' ann an cèo
O thalla, a ghalair, is tilleadh mo bhèo!

Nar bheil fuath agam air m' obair
Ach tha gràin agam air sgìths
Le bhith fulang leis a' ghalar-clèibh,
Tha mi deònach a chur sìos!

O is garbh an sgleò, is mis' ann an cèo
O thalla, a ghalair, is tilleadh mo bhèo!

2 Ruined Relic of my Health

Ruined relic of my health upon the fields
Coughing and snivelling all the long day
Ho a ho be away, I am tormented
Ho a ho be away, be well, well away!

Three hankies and cuppas and three whiskies
The sneezing's a snorting, 't will be my ruination
Ho a ho be away, be completely away,
The devil and evil be upon you, bronchitis!

3 Rime of Imprisonment in Illness

O fierce is the contest, and I am confused
O be away, illness, and let me return to life!

I am not indisposed to work
But this fatigue disgusts me
As for suffering with bronchitis,
I am more than happy to curse it!

O fierce is the contest, and I am confused
O be away, illness, and let me return to life!

29 Aillse

Am facal fhèin
na thul-ionnsaigh
buille-cuisle air chall
buille-cridhe oillt:
chan fhaod a bhith.
Tuaineal ceòtha gil orm
eagal maoim pian deòir
rùisgte leònte air mo dhlò.

Mo bheatha
air thiolp leis a' chuairteig
gam thilg is chuibhleadh
le fòirneart mun cuairt
gam fhàgail gun fhèin-fhiosrachd
gun roghainn, gun smachd.

Cha tàinig sìon gu tìr
far an deach a reubadh,
ach sgaoilte air thuaiream
air feadh fearainn mhùithte.

Gach faoineas air sguabadh,
ach brìgh nithean luachmhor
soillseach seunta ath-shuaicheanta
cruinne ùr neo-aithnichte dhomh:
ach nach àlainn so-leònte iongantach
a bhoidhchead?

29 Cancer

The very word
an absolute assault
a missed pulse
heartdrumbeat horror:
it cannot be.
Stupefied by white mist
fear panic pain tears
naked wounded alone.

My life
snatched up by the vortex
hurling and whirling me
violently about
depriving me of consciousness
of choice, of control.

Not one single thing fell back to earth
where it was ripped up,
but scattered in random fashion
on altered terrain.

All vain things swept away,
only the meaning of the worthwhile
in luminous numinous fresh significance
a new world unrecognizable to me:
yet is not its lovely fragile beauty
wonderful?

Agus buidheachas orm
a bhith beò is mar-aon riut
a thog tro shàr-dheuchainn
an teine-leaghaidh mi,
gu camhanaich eile
gu daingeann ri mo thaobh
led shùil air reul-iùil
còrr ar beatha.

And I am grateful
to be alive and at one with you
who carried me through the sore ordeal
of the refiner's fire,
towards a different dawn
steadfast by my side
your gaze fixed on the lodestar
of the balance of our lives.

30 Cò bu mhise

Bha cianalas orm
air mo shon fhìn
às dèidh taisteil
thar chrìochan an fhulangais.

Bha mi air dol seacharan
is mì-chinnt breislich orm
cò bu mhise roimhe,
no às ùr.

Bha mi gam ionndrainn fhìn,
m' aighearachd m' aotromachd m' ait
is mi a' sireadh m' anam air ais.

Ciamar sa chruinne-chè
a gheibhinn dhachaigh
ach a' tarraing air ràmhan
mo churachain bhig fhìn? –
tarsainn air abhainn Lethe
gus an ruiginn
mo dhìochuimhne
leis an rithim-iomraidh
a rèiticheas.

30 Who I was - and would be

I was homesick
for myself
after a journey
beyond suffering's boundary.

I went missing
with dementing uncertainty
of who I was before,
or might be anew.

I missed myself,
my playfulness, lightness, my joy
and longed to have my soul back.

How in the wide world
would I reach home
other than by pulling on the oars
of my own little coracle? –
across the river Lethe
until I could reach
my forgetting
with the rowing-rhythm
that reconciles.

31 An Dàrna Leth

Ro-chluich:
'S e mo shlighe neo-thaghte, chan e mo dhàn
ach fhuair mi manadh oirre 's mi òg.
Seachad air leth-cheud a-nis,
Tuigidh mi an eirmse:
Bha iomadh faileas mealltach sa chiad leth.

Rann 1:
'Ma tha thu a' sireadh toradh, dèan do dhìcheall.'
Bidh an t-ubhal as fheàrr air a' mheangan as àirde...
Is sin a dh'fheuch mi, is shoirbhich leam
Sa chiad shreath. 'S fhad o mo bhrèith
Bha 'n dàrna leth, an dàrna leth.

Rann 2:
'Chan eil sealbh no soirbheas air an gealladh.'
Cha sheas an àbhaist an còmhnaidh...
M' athair caillte is mi ach nam nighinn
Làithean caochlaideach, 's dh'fhulaing mi cràdh
Là fuar no teth, an-diugh no 'n-dè,
Ron dàrna leth, ron dàrna leth.

31 The Second Half

Prelude:
It is not a path I chose, nor is it fate,
Yet I had a premonition of it when young.
Past fifty now,
I understand the whimsy:
Shadows and delusions a-plenty in the first half.

Verse 1:
'If you want to succeed, make an honest effort.'
The finest apple is on the highest branch...
And so I did, and it succeeded
In the first stage. Yet a far distance from birth
Was the second half, the second half.

Verse 2:
'But good fortune or success are not guaranteed.'
Nothing stays the same...
With my father lost to me when still but a girl,
In treacherous times that inflicted pain
Whether the day was cold day or warm, yesterday or morrow
Before the second half, the second half.

Rann 3:

'Thig misneachd is cofhurtachd às dèidh fulangais is cràidh.'
Neach gun dà là, neach gun là idir...
A' cumail mo dhòchais, an oidhirp, 's m' iùl
Thàinig cùisean gu buil, nochd càirdeas is spèis
'S mi a' leantail mo shlighe, fiù 's
Mur eil i rèidh, fon ghrèin is fo dheigh
San dàrna leth, san dàrna leth.

Rann 4:

'Fàsaidh an ùine agad nas gainne, ach nas prìseile dhut'
Nam bu bhuan, bu mhaith...
Fhathast falaichte ge be dè tha romham,
Ach gun fhiosta 's mi a' fàs nas daingne
Agus nas sàsaicht' sa chuibhreann gu crìoch.
Aig fois is gun aithreachas thèid
Mo theicheadh à crè gu luaithre an dèidh
Mo dhàrna leth, mo dhàrna leth.

Iar-chluich:

Lem shùilean air fairge an dàrna leth
Ach gun chinnt air a' mheud
'S e mo thaghadh-sa, mo chuid 's mo rath
Tlachd is sòlas a thogail 's a thairgsinn
Anns gach ceàrnaidh is oisean rim bheò.
Chì mi nas fharsainge sa chuibhrean seo
Agus 's e sealladh bòidheach a th' ann.

Verse 3:
'Better spirits and comfort will follow suffering and pain.'
A person who has had no ups and downs has not lived...
Maintaining hopes, efforts and aims
There were accomplishments, affection, respect,
So I still followed my path, even when
Far from smooth, whether in sun or ice,
In the second half, the second half.

Verse 4:
'Your time is becoming scarcer but more precious to you.'
It would be good were it to last...
Though whatever lies ahead is still hidden,
Yet unconsciously, I grow steadier
And more contented, in the final allocated span.
At peace and without regrets I shall
Vanish from clay to ash, after
My second half, my second half.

Postlude:
With my gaze on the horizon of the second half
But uncertain of its length,
It is now my choice, my role and my fortune
To find and to offer joy and comfort
In every nook and corner of my life.
I can see further in this, my remaining span,
And the view is beautiful.

32 Easbhaidh

Thusa fo iomagain
eagal ort
ro easbhaidh

easbhaidh fharsaing
ioma-fhillte
bagarrach:
thèid do shealg
le eagal easbhaidh,
feadh do throm-laighe,
a dh'ionnsaigh na camhanaich

iomagaineach
gun a bhith
math gu leòr
treun gu leòr
sèimh gu leòr;
gun a bhith
airidh air aire
meas, gaol, àigh

Ge-tà
bi cinnteach
gu bheil thu sàbhailte
bi sìthte
a bhith beò, tèarainte, prìseil

32 Deficiency

You are anxious
In fear of
deficiency

far-reaching deficiency
multi-faceted
threatening:
you are hunted
by fear of falling short,
through your nightmares,
towards dawn's light

anxious
of not being
good enough
brave enough
kind enough;
of not being
worthy of notice
respect, love, joy.

And yet
be assured
that you are safe
be contented
to be alive, secure, valued

dìth easbhaidh fa dheòidh
pailteas, beairteas
d' fhòghnas agad
òir d' fhòghnas annad fhèin.

an absence of deficiencies at last
plenty, riches
you have sufficient
for you are your own sufficiency.

VIII Anam-charaid

33 An aileag a bh' air Aristophanes

Chuir i dàil seachd bliadhna oirnn,
an aileag a bh' air Aristophanes –
aileag cridhealais-dùrachd –
's sinne gun fhiost' a' feitheamh
aig snaidhm-rathaid ar beatha

ach shoirbhich leis
a sgeul faoin-mhilis innse
mu dhaoine spealgte
ann an dà chruinn leth
is a' caoidh an cèile

is dh'aidich sinne ar gràdh
thachair sinn rinne fa dheòidh
is fhuair sinne a chèile
le deòin di-beathte
ar snaidhm-cridhe –

eadar-fhigheadh ar n-anam
snaidhm-beatha – co-bhann ar teachd
snaidhm-aonachd
snaidhm ar seuna
snaidhm-sinne

VIII Soulmate

33 Aristophanes' bout of the hiccups

they delayed us for seven years
Aristophanes' bout of the hiccups
merrily serious hiccups
while we waited, unaware,
at the road-knot of our lives

but he did contrive to tell
his whimsical-sweet story
of people cloven
into two neat half-spheres
and missing their other half

and we confessed our love
we finally happened
and received each other
with willing welcome
of our intertwined hearts –

inter-weaving of our souls
knot of life – binding our future
knot of unity
knot of our enchantment
knot of the pair of us

snaidhmte ri chèile
aig co-imleag ar gaoil,
sàr-bhuailte le beithir
ar rath suaib-chuthaich
ach le cinnt aighearraich
snaidhm a chur nach fhuasgladh.

An t-iar-fhacal: Aileag-dùrachd ... gu aileag cridhealais

An aileag a bh' air Aristophanes
Thug i maill' oirnn fad' seachd bliadhn'
Ach thairgeadh cruinne-chè gealltanais
Is dhìobradh teagamh is fiamh.

knotted together
at the navel of our love
sorely smitten by the thunderbolt of happen-chance
slightly-touched-by-madness
but with joyful certainty
of tying a knot that cannot be loosed.

Epilogue: Serious hiccups ... to merry hiccups

Aristophanes' bout of the hiccups
That delayed us for seven years
Bestowed a universe of promise
And banished all doubts and fears.

34 Sneachd a' Ghiblein

Bleòiteagan-sneachda
a' sgiathalaich sìos
gam shuathachadh gu h-aotrom
gam shlìobadh
mar iteag:

mar do mheuran
do-thuigsinn tlùsail
a' cluich air cruit mo cholainn
agus do ghaol do-chreidsinn caomh
mar cheòl nan teud
nam chridhe.

34 April Snow

Small snow-flakes
drifting down
touching me lightly
stroking me
like a little feather:

like your fingers
with unimaginable tenderness
playing upon the harp of my body
and your love surpassingly kind
is the harpstrings' song
in my heart.

35 Reachd

Dithis dhaoine ciallach
aig meadhan am beatha
agus air dùil a thrèigsinn –
ma dh'fhaoidhte –
mean air mhean,
a bhith am feast
nan ceist-ri-ceist.

Ach thuit sinn
ann an gràdh domhainn,
agus le roileasg
dhòchasach
shiubhail sinn
fo iùl fuil-taisgealaiche
gu àilean sàsaichte,
air ar glacadh
le reachd.[32]

Mise fo fhasgadh d' achlais
dìon draoidheil orm
do chùram gam thàladh
is sinne fo sheun
fiughair foirfe.

35 RaptureRegulation

Two sensible people
in their mid-life
who'd abandoned expectations –
it might perhaps be –
little by little,
of ever again being
lover-loved.

And yet we have fallen
deeply in love,
and in a confusion
of joyous hope
we have journeyed
guided by our discoverer-blood
to an oasis of contentment,
taken captive
by rapture.

I in the shelter of your arms
magically protected
lulled by your caring
and both of us under the spell
of a perfect hopefulness.

---

32 Reachd in Gaelic has two strikingly different meanings: 'passion' and 'orderliness'.

Nach iongantach
nach eil sinn
air dol gu tur seacharan
air dol às ar rian sean-reachdail
le reachd
ar gaoil ùir?

Is it not strange
that we have not
gone completely astray
and parted company with our orderly old senses
deranged by the power
of our newfound love?

36 Reudan

thusa a tha sona
ann an saoghal leat fhèin
do mhacmeanma beò-dhaithte
do smuaintean a' dannsadh
reudan a th' annad.
cuairsgeach
am broinn seann leabhair
air duilleag cnag na sgeulachd,
an duilleag as tàlaidhiche dhut,
gàire aoibhneis air d' aodann.

ciamar san t-saoghal
a thogainn d' aire
reudain chòir
gus do tharraing ann an còmhradh –
saoil, a ghràidh?

shnàgainn san leabhar
am falach eadar na duilleagan
a' feitheamh ort.
nì mi comharra-duilleag
asam fhìn.
is nuair a thachras tu rium
gheibh thu iongnadh
gheibh thu pòg bhuam
gheibh thu mise
mar leabhar-chèile
bho seo a-mach.

36 Bookworm

you are so contented
in a world of your own
your imagination colourfully alive
your thoughts dancing
such a bookworm.
curled up
inside an old book
on the page with the nub of the story,
the page that most entices you,
a smile of happiness on your face.

how in the world
might I attract your attention,
beloved bookworm
and draw you into conversation –
how do you imagine, darling?

I would sneak into the book
hidden between the pages
and lie in wait for you.
I will reinvent myself
as a bookmark.
and when you happen upon me
you'll get a surprise
you'll receive a kiss from me
and you'll have me
as your book-companion
from now on.

Crotal Ruadh – Red Lichen

Sandaidh NicDhòmhnaill Jones

Leas-phàipear – Annex: Na Fuinn – The Tunes

Òran 1	Na Fir-Chlis – 'The Nimble Ones' – The Northern Lights
Òran 5	Òran Chòisir nan Gàidheal – The Song of the Gaelic Choirs
Òran 6	An Togarrachd Fhaoin – Futile Wishfulness
Òran 7	Gealach an Abachaidh – Harvest Moon
Òran 8	Tìr a' mhurain – Land of the marram-grass
Òran 9	Uibhist Fhuranach – The Welcome of Uist
Òran 10	Dàn Buan-Bhuidheachais – The Song of Eternal Gratitude

Òran 1 Na Fir-Chlis - 'The Nimble Ones' - The Northern Lights

Bàrdachd agus Fonn/Lyrics and Music le Sandaidh NicDhòmhnaill Jones

Òran 5 Òran Chòisir nan Gàidheal - The Song of the Gaelic Choirs

Mar chomharrachadh air sia fichead bliadhna a' Chomuinn Ghàidhealaich

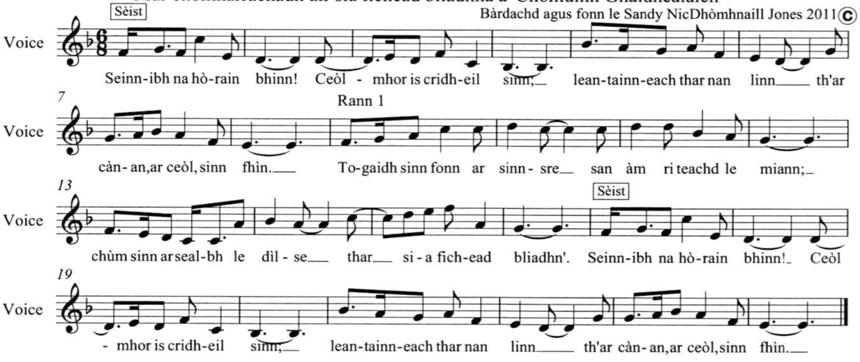

Òran 6 An Togarrachd Fhaoin - Futile Wishfulness

Bàrdachd agus fonn le Sandy NicDhòmhnaill Jones 2009 ©

Òran 7 Gealach an Abachaidh - Harvest Moon

Bàrdachd agus Fonn le Sandy NicDhòmhnaill Jones 2010 ©

Òran 8 Tìr a' mhurain - Land of the marram-grass

Bàrdachd agus fonn le Sandy NicDhòmhnaill Jones 2007 ©

Òran 9 Uibhist Fhuranach - The Welcome of Uist

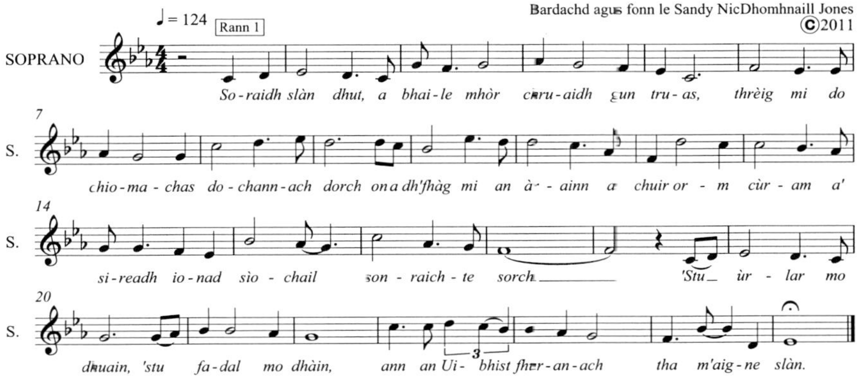

Òran 10 Dàn Buan-Bhuidheachais - The Song of Eternal Gratitude